Il Trovatore

BLACK DOG OPERA LIBRARY

Il Trovatore

GIUSEPPE VERDI
TEXT BY ROBERT LEVINE

BLACK DOG
& LEVENTHAL
PUBLISHERS
NEW YORK

Published by
Black Dog & Leventhal Publishers, Inc.
151 West 19th Street
New York, NY 10011

Distributed by
Workman Publishing Company
708 Broadway
New York, NY 10003

Designed by Alleycat Design, Inc.

Photo Research: Anne Burns Images

Manufactured in **Singapore**

ISBN: 1-57912-066-0

h g f e d c b

FOREWORD

*G*ypsies and troubadors, love and revenge all characterize *Il Trovatore*: one of the most memorable of Verdi's masterworks. Brooding reminiscences and thundering orchestration surround the famous Anvil Chorus in this opera which came right at the midpoint of Verdi's career. *Trovatore* has a style of its own, unique in its dark melodrama and tragic plot developments.

You will hear the entire opera on the two compact discs included on the inside front and back covers of this book. As you explore the text, you will discover the story behind the opera and its creation, the background of the composer, biographies of the principal singers and conductor, and the opera's libretto, both in the original Italian and in an English translation. Special commentary has been included throughout the libretto to aid in your appreciation and highlight key moments in the action and score.

Enjoy this book and enjoy the music.

OTHER TITLES IN THE SERIES

ABOUT THE AUTHOR

*R*obert Levine is a New York based music and travel writer whose work has appeared in dozens of newspapers and periodicals around the world. In addition to his being Senior Classical Music Advisor to Amazon.com, he contributes to *Stereophile, Fanfare, Opera News* and *BBC Music Magazine* and acts as advisor to a handful of European opera companies and artists.

ACKNOWLEDGEMENTS

The author would like to thank Paul Harrington for his help in preparing the manuscript.

GIUSEPPE VERDI, (1813-1901)

Il Trovatore

There is no doubt that Wagner, Mozart and Giuseppe Verdi (1813-1901) make up the triumvirate of the world's greatest opera composers. From the moment his third opera, *Nabucco*, was produced at La Scala in 1842, Verdi's reputation in Italy was made, and with his next pair of operas, *I Lombardi alla Prima Crociata* and *Ernani*, he gained renown and respect all over Europe.

During the next few years he turned out operas quickly and efficiently: *I Due Foscari, Giovanna d'Arco, Alzira, Attila, Macbeth, I Masnadieri, Jérusalem* (a reworking of *I Lombardi* for Paris), *Il Corsaro, La Battaglia di Legnano, Luisa Miller* and *Stiffelio.* These works, some excellent (*Macbeth, Luisa Miller*), some duds (*Alzira, Il Corsaro*), Verdi composed during what he referred to as "my years in the galley." He was learning—indeed, perfecting—his craft, while garnering more and more celebrity.

Despite his growing fame and the success of *Rigoletto*, which has come to

Conte di Luna

Trovatore
Metropolitan Verdi
Opera 69

Attilio Colonnello
68

COSTUME SKETCH FOR THE COUNT DI LUNA, METROPOLITAN OPERA, 1968

signify the beginning of the fecund "middle period" of his career, 1851 was not an easy year in Giuseppe Verdi's life. He was living openly with soprano Giuseppina Strepponi, which scandalized his home town and particularly his parents. Tension between the elder Verdis and Giuseppina rose to such levels that Giuseppe bought his parents a house outside town and moved them there. Despite the concern of his friends and family, the two continued living together for another eight years before they finally married. Verdi's seemingly libertine personal life was not the only thing that scandalized the public. On the professional front, people were also shocked (and given his successes, tantalized as well) by what seemed rather prurient subject matter in his operas, such as the rape in *Rigoletto*.

Luckily for posterity, Verdi was not unused to adversity. His first wife, Margherita, and their two infant children had died in 1840. At the same time, his second opera, *Un giorno di regno*, flopped. Nevertheless, he managed to persevere and establish himself in the ensuing decade as a significant figure in Italian music, and through his music, in politics. He was very much an unflinching, self-made man, and his successes reflect this.

Born the son of an innkeeper in the village of Roncole in 1813, Verdi began his musical education at a very young age. His parents encouraged his interest in music and early on gave him his own little spinet. He studied organ, and by age seven was organist at San Michele Arcangelo, his parish church. In 1823 Verdi moved to the neighboring town of Busseto. Although a small town, Busseto had a Philharmonic Society and a music school, which Verdi attended. Busseto's close proximity to his home town allowed him to continue playing organ at San Michele while attending the music school. By the age of 14, besides maintaining his position in Roncole, he was teaching the younger pupils, and composing marches and other types of music under the headmaster's guidance.

At 18, after finishing the four-year music school in Busseto, Verdi moved into the home of Antonio Barezzi, a local merchant and patron of music. Barezzi made it financially possible for Verdi to apply for admission to the prestigious Milan Conservatory, but curiously, Verdi's talents were found wanting; he was rejected for admission and advised to seek a private tutor. Verdi found Vincenzo Lavigna, an opera composer who also conducted at La Scala. An excellent musician in his own right, Lavigna taught Verdi counterpoint and introduced him to Milan. Perhaps even more important was Lavigna's contact with La Scala, for it was this relationship that enabled Verdi to make his name.

In 1836 Verdi returned to Busseto and gained the post of *maestro di musica* of the Philharmonic. Soon after, he married Margherita, the daughter of his patron. In Busseto, he continued to compose operas, and in 1839, on the recommendation of the soprano (his future lover) Giuseppina Strepponi and others who recognized the young composer's worth, the manager of La Scala decided to stage Verdi's first opera, *Oberto, Conte di San Bonifacio.*

Verdi's earliest operas were much in the form of and used the conventions of the *bel canto* style which Donizetti, Bellini and Rossini epitomized. But he worked to develop and alter these structures for the sake of verisimilitude, eventually creating highly individual and dramatic works of art through his experimentation not only with structure, but also with harmony and orchestration.

Interest in playing with the operatic form was on Verdi's mind when he first read Antonio García Gutièrrez's *El Trovador.* The strong situations and characters, especially the gypsy Azucena, fired his imagination: Verdi saw in the bizarre plot and insane passions of the protagonists a pretext for operatic boldness. Originally performed in 1836, the play thrilled audiences with its power and originality, and the 23-year-old playwright immediately became famous. (A disciple of Victor Hugo,

Gutièrrez was also influenced by a fellow Spaniard, the Duke of Rivas, and in particular by his play *Don Alvaro o La Fuerza Destino*, which a few years later Verdi turned into *La forza del destino*.)

The librettist Salvadore Cammarano, on instructions from Verdi, acquired a copy of the play and set to work turning it into a libretto. In his enthusiasm for

VERDI, SEATED AT CENTER, SURROUNDED BY FRIENDS AND COLLEAGUES.
LEFT TO RIGHT: SIGNORA CARRARA-STOLTZ, GIUSEPPINA STREPPONI, UNIDENTIFIED WOMAN, CLEOFONTE CAMPANINI, VERDI, GIULIO AND GIUDITTA RICORDI AND AN UNIDENTIFIED MAN.

The world's great music is on Victor Red Seal Records

LoveAmong Battlements

THE "MISERERE" +
FROM · IL TROVATORE

COVER ILLUSTRATION FROM A RED SEAL RECORDS ALBUM OF IL TROVATORE

18

what was to become *Il trovatore*, Verdi wrote to a friend, "The more Cammarano provides me with originality and freedom of form, the better I shall be able to do." He was interested in exploring an operatic ideal "in which there were neither cavatinas, nor duets, nor trios, nor choruses...and the whole opera was (if I might express it this way) one single piece." This statement was tantamount to a manifesto against the *bel canto* operas; Verdi wanted realism "or as much of it as the censors would permit" and saw that one road to it was by revolutionizing the form, which then consisted of set pieces: for example, aria followed by cabaletta.

Cammarano had his work cut out for him. Gutièrrez's *El Trovador* is a work of unbridled Romantic passions. The three leading characters, Leonor (Leonora), Manrique (Manrico) and Don Nuno (Count di Luna) pay heed to nothing but their own wild emotions. As if that were not enough of a challenge, the original work was similar to Elizabethan drama, written partly in prose and partly in verse. Although this would be a significant test of the poetic nature of a libretto, it is not as major a factor as the changes Cammarano and Verdi made in the opera's *dramatis personae*.

In the opera, the character of Leonora's brother is cut entirely, and the emphasis put on Azucena, a gypsy woman torn between love for her son and her desire to avenge her mother's death. That Verdi's own mother had died not long after he moved his parents into their new home (away from Giuseppina) might explain the sympathy he had for Azucena from the very beginning of his work on the opera. The importance of Azucena to the drama was a matter he continually urged upon Cammarano. For the final act, he suggested to Cammarano, "Don't make Azucena go mad. Exhausted with fatigue, suffering, terror and sleeplessness, she speaks confusedly. Her faculties are weakened, but she is not mad. This woman's two great passions, her love for Manrico and her wild desire to avenge her mother, must be sustained to the end." To Verdi, Azucena was the leading character in the play, and he made sure she was revealed with great compassion.

Unfortunately, Cammarano did not—at first—appear up to Verdi's challenge. Set against a backdrop of a 15th-century Spanish Civil War, Gutièrrez's play is a gigantic historical melodrama. Cammarano had to contend with complicated politics and a sprawling plot. The librettist sent a draft synopsis to Verdi not long before the premiere of *Rigoletto*. On April 9, 1851, just a month after that premiere, Verdi replied to Cammarano, "I have read your sketch. As a gifted and most exceptional man, you will not be offended if I humbly take the liberty of saying it would be better to give up this subject if we cannot manage to retain all the boldness and novelty of the Spanish play."

The final result of Cammarano's efforts is thought by detractors to be somewhat difficult to follow. For many it is the epitome of the confused and silly operatic libretto of the Romantic period. Gilbert and Sullivan parodied the baby-switching in *The Gondoliers*, and it is *Il trovatore* which is mocked in the Marx Brothers' *A Night at the Opera*. Unfortunately, this appraisal is close to the truth. The plot is complicated and full of what might generously be termed magical realism, and important actions (baby-burnings, kidnappings, duels, executions) take place either before the opera or off-stage. But on an emotional level, it packs a wallop. Cammarano managed, ultimately, to craft from the truly unwieldy canvas of the original play a viable romantic melodrama which merely pushes one's suspension of disbelief. Of course, the way Verdi's music clarifies and crystallizes emotions takes the plot to a whole other dimension.

Verdi and Giuseppina spent the winter of 1851-1852 in Paris. There Verdi had begun to work on a musical setting for the play which Alexander Dumas *fils* had adapted from his novel, *La Dame aux Camélias* (ultimately, *La traviata*). While

LUCIANO PAVAROTTI (MANRICO) AND
JOAN SUTHERLAND (LEONORA) IN A
METROPOLITAN OPERA PRODUCTION, 1987

there, Verdi also signed a contract to write a new work for production at the Paris Opéra two years later. This announcement led to a request from Vienna for *Trovatore*, coupled with a hint that Verdi might be appointed to the post of *Hofkapellmeister*, which Donizetti had once held. At this time Verdi offered to replace *Il trovatore* with the Dumas play, but Cammarano decided to persevere in his work. For his part, Verdi put aside *La Dame aux Camélias*, and concentrated upon *Il trovatore*.

Despite the renewed enthusiasm with which the two men approached the work, it took quite a bit longer to finish. Not only was his father ill, but Cammarano also was ill when he began the commission, and he died in Naples in July of 1852. "I was thunderstruck by the sad news of Cammarano. I can't describe the depth of my sorrow. I read of his death not in a letter from a friend but in a stupid theatrical journal. You loved him as I did, and will understand the feelings I cannot find words for. Poor Cammarano. What a loss," wrote Verdi to their mutual friend, Cesare de Sanctis.

Part of the third and all of the fourth act of the libretto remained unwritten, but Verdi paid Cammerano's widow 600 ducats instead of the agreed upon 500. Through de Sanctis he engaged a young Neapolitan poet, Leone Emanuele Bardare, to sort out Cammarano's notes and complete the work, but there was still no concern for the opera's timeliness, as it had not yet been commissioned by anyone. Verdi had suggested it to Cammarano because he loved the play; he was at a point in his career where he no longer had to worry about having an opera accepted for performance. He had intended to offer it to the San Carlo in Naples because of Cammarano's connections there; however, his main concern was that the opera be staged in the theater which had the most suitable singers for it. Finally, he decided to allow the first production to be staged by

BRONZE BUST OF VERDI, WHICH IS HOUSED IN MILAN'S FAMOUS LA SCALA OPERA HOUSE

the Apollo Theater in Rome, and to premiere on January 19, 1853.

Verdi also agreed to have *La traviata* ready for performance at the Fenice in Venice on March 6, so while he was rehearsing *Il trovatore* in Rome, he was composing *La traviata*. It is said that once Bardare delivered the completed libretto, Verdi took only a month (November, 1852) to compose *Il trovatore*. It may be true that he put pen to paper in November, but he had been working on the opera in his head for almost a year, and his work certainly showed. The premiere in January was an overwhelming success. The Gazzeta Musicale reported: "The composer deserved this splendid triumph, for he has here written music in a new style, imbued with Castilian characteristics. The public listened to each number in religious silence, breaking out into applause at every interval, the end of the third act and the whole of the fourth arousing such enthusiasm that their repetition was demanded."

Il trovatore's immediate success in Rome led to performances across the globe. Critics were not uniform in their praise, however; several complained that Verdi was killing off the art of *bel canto* by the impossible demands he made on his singers. Others objected to the violence and gloom of the plot. "People say the opera is too sad, and that there are too many deaths in it," wrote Verdi to the Countess Maffei. "But, after all, death is all there is in life. What else is there?"

The pessimistic over-dramatizing that seems to have been one of Verdi's natural characteristics is certainly reflected in *Il trovatore*. Its story is the very height of Romantic drama: Before the opera's action begins, a Count charges a gypsy woman with witchcraft because he believes she has cursed his son, and has her burned at the stake. As she dies she calls out to her daughter, Azucena, "Avenge me!" Soon after, the girl kidnaps the Count's child and in a confused, muddled rage, throws him upon a fire, then passes out. When Azucena comes to, she realizes that in her addled state she has burned her own son, and so adopts the Count's son as her own.

The opera begins several years later, when Leonora, lady-in-waiting to the Princess of Aragon, is awaiting her lover, a mysterious troubadour. While she is in love with this sexy stranger, the Count di Luna (brother of the baby Azucena kidnapped years ago and raised as her own son) is madly in love with her. Di Luna comes across Leonora just as his rival has begun serenading her. When the enigmatic singer reveals himself as Manrico, a wanted follower of a nobleman who is rebelling against the Princess, a duel ensues (offstage) and Manrico defeats di Luna. From there things snowball dramatically. The Count's jealousy drives him crazy, Leonora and Manrico both die (one by suicide, the other execution) and it is Azucena who lives, although her survival is hardly a piece of good news. Ultimately, gloom pervades all.

In Verdi's pursuit of Romantic perfection, *Il trovatore* is a wonderful, ecstatic tumult of emotionalism. Interestingly, it is in the opera's emotional extremism that the characters and situations clarify themselves. While many critics charged that the opera was the death of *bel canto*, it might be said that the opera's demand for vocal beauty, agility and range, it is the very glorification of the genre. While this approach would seem to create an opera in which one-dimensional characters belt out impassioned arias, Verdi masterfully used this method to expose his characters and make them more compelling. Verdi isolates the story and his characters within the arias. The recitatives, where the plot of an opera is usually revealed, play

Antica sede della Casa editrice G. Ricordi e C. nell'edificio del Teatro alla Scala di Milano

THE ORIGINAL HEADQUARTERS OF G. RICORDI PUBLISHING, ATTACHED TO THE SIDE OF LA SCALA

a less significant role. Verdi did not, in fact, destroy *bel canto*, he merely took it to another level. In the character and vocal line of Azucena, he also created the first character in opera who might be at home in the *verismo* works of Mascagni and Leoncavallo, almost a half century later.

The opera's brief 27 bars of orchestral introduction range from softly rumbling drum rolls to clarion-like horn blasts, setting the stage for the beating of passionate hearts and the warlike scenes we are about to witness. The mood thus set, the opera begins with Ferrando's (Count di Luna's lieutenant) recounting of the burning of

THE METROPOLITAN OPERA CHORUS IN IL TROVATORE, 1998

the gypsy and the kidnapping of the current Count's older brother. His vocal line requires the agility associated with *bel canto*, but the delivery is far more rough-and-tumble. We meet Leonora in the following scene. Leonora is Verdi's most Mozartian heroine: Her arias possess the stature and elegance of the Countess Almaviva's in *The Marriage of Figaro*, calling for a style in performance reaching beyond *bel canto* to 18th-century formality. Her *"Tacea la notte"* in the first act is one of Verdi's most memorable soprano arias and tells us everything we should know about her: She represents all things lyrical in *Il trovatore*; she is a beautiful aristocrat who expresses herself in graceful melody.

Azucena is the antithesis of Leonora's exquisite nobility: She is a common gypsy, a woman of the earth. Lyrical in fits and starts, Azucena is Verdi's first important mezzo-soprano role. While Leonora is deeply in love with Manrico, and that love ultimately leads to her sacrificing herself for him, her life is relatively uncomplicated. On the other hand, Azucena has lived her life with her mother's "Avenge me!" echoing in her mind, and every day she must look at Manrico (her "son") remembering that because of him her mother was killed and she accidentally incinerated her own son. While we barely listen to Leonora's words—sung properly, the sound of her aria is so beautiful, who can be troubled to pay attention to what she's actually saying?—we cannot help being drawn to the fascinating and compelling things Azucena says. When she begins her second-act narrative, alone with Manrico (*"Condotta ell'era in ceppi"*) in which she recounts the terrible events of her mother's death, one is compelled to follow every madly delivered word.

In Count di Luna we quickly recognize a nobleman. Despite his growing jealous fury throughout the opera, his finely nuanced arias remind us of his aristocratic birth. Verdi was careful not to have Azucena go insane at the end, but it is clear he never had any such intention for di Luna. In the first lines of the opera

VERDI

Par G. PILOTELL

CARICATURE OF
VERDI BY GEORGES
LABADIE PILOTELL
(1844-1918)

we are told by his soldiers that he compulsively spends his nights under Leonora's balcony. By the second scene of Act II, we see hints of madness: Leonora, thinking di Luna has killed Manrico in battle, has decided to join a convent. Di Luna comes to the convent to stop her, even if he has to use force. He sings an aria of great tenderness exclaiming his love for Leonora which is followed immediately by a fierce declaration that not even God will stop him from having her. In this scene Verdi invented a new type of baritone role, using the baritone's range as he would a tenor's: di Luna's high Gs have the climactic effect of a tenor's B flat. Combined with breathless rhythms and dramatic variations from soft to loud and back again, this underlines the Count's desperate state of mind. Di Luna is not evil; rather, he is simply a man whose obsession with Leonora has driven him crazy.

Despite the fact that Manrico is indeed di Luna's brother, he was raised by Azucena as a gypsy, and his offstage song in the second scene of Act I, *"Deserto sulla terra,"* reflects both his elegance and his earthiness. A truly romantic figure, Manrico is forceful, as one would expect from one with his gypsy background, yet as courtly as any nobleman. Throughout the opera he is driven back and forth attempting to court Leonora or save his mother, and his music constantly reflects this dichotomy. In his great third-act aria, *"Ah, si ben mio,"* he lyrically—read aristocratically—assures Leonora that his strength comes from her love, and that if he should die, they will meet again in heaven. This triumph of *bel canto* (Verdi even wrote in a trill for the tenor) is interrupted by news that Azucena is in danger, and Manrico's vocal line changes style entirely: He firmly, wildly and earthily promises to defend or die with his mother, as if there were nothing else he could, should or would be doing. (This is also one of the great tenor showpieces in opera, and although Verdi did not write either of the high Cs you will hear in this recording, he did approve them "if the tenor was good enough.")

And so we see that while di Luna is driven mad by his passion, Manrico is driven to the grave by the conflicting love for his mother and lover.

The opera's intense—at times berserk—theatricality comes crashing home in its final act, where we again witness both the *bel canto* and the new Verdian approach. The act opens outside the tower in which Manrico and Azucena are imprisoned (their capture, a pivotal point in the plot, has occurred offstage, seemingly during intermission). Leonora's ravishing aria, *"D'amor sull' ali rosee,"* in which she again proclaims her love for Manrico, while hoping he does not feel her misery, is filled with the beauty and poignancy which personifies her. The *"Miserere,"* in which monks chant for those about to die, is intertwined with the troubadour's own song of heart-broken ecstasy and is a great *coup de théâtre*—the gloom with which it pervades the stage is almost Herculean. Leonora then declares her intention to either save-

AZUCENA ON HER KNEES, METROPOLITAN OPERA, 1987

him or die with him—neither of which would be out of character. Di Luna's entrance allows for a stirring duet in which Leonora agrees to give herself to the Count in return for Manrico's life. The Count gloats characteristically as Leonora surreptitiously takes poison. *"M'avrai, ma fredda, esanime spoglia (You'll have me, but I'll be a lifeless corpse!)"* she exclaims to herself and us, in her darkest vocal register. Let's face it, melodrama doesn't get much better than this.

In the final scene, we overhear (or at least that is the superbly dramatic impression) Manrico tenderly—in a melody long and graceful enough to have been composed by Bellini—singing his chronically terrified mother to sleep. Leonora rushes in to tell her love that he will be freed. Manrico suspiciously and angrily wonders what price she must have paid for his release, but just as he has figured out the nature of the bargain she made with the Count, she falls dead at his feet. Di Luna enters, sees Leonora dead and orders Manrico to be executed immediately. Azucena wakes up and is forced by di Luna to watch Manrico's death. Just seconds too late to save him, she tells the Count that he has killed his own brother, and in a final phrase, rising to her top B flat, Azucena cries, *"Sei vendicata, o madre (You are avenged, mother)."* The Count realizes he is doomed to live with this horrible knowledge, as the curtain falls on what must either be taken seriously or not at all.

And, of course, it is taken seriously,

THE LIBRETTO, SHOWING THE FIRST FEW BARS OF "ABBIETTA ZINGARA," THE OPERA'S FIRST ARIA

not because we have any way of relating to the situations in which the characters find themselves, but because of the extraordinary range of Verdi's music. We might have had some disbelief issues with the setting initially—serenading troubadours, mad, passionate noblemen, flaming babies, almost—entry into a convent—but *Il trovatore* sneaks up on the listener and becomes credible almost subliminally. Midway, we have accepted and begun to look forward to Manrico's musical heroism, Leonora's dulcet empathy and fidelity, the Count's musically mood-swinging lunacy and Azucena's maddening confusion, exhibited in her jagged and far-flung vocal lines. *Il trovatore* works because Verdi gets us in the gut through his music, which is as clear as the plot is not—and music is more universal and instinctual than text.

A century ago, there was no doubt that *Il trovatore* was Verdi's most popular work. In 1862 the composer wrote to his friend Count Arrivabene, "Should you go to the Indies or the heart of Africa, you will always hear *Il trovatore.*" Countless parodies of the opera during the period showed this to be true, as did the sound of the "Anvil Chorus" (Act 2, scene 1) on barrel organs and street pianos throughout the world. Despite our modern age's discomfort with such arch-Romanticism, *Il trovatore* remains an important part of the operatic repertoire.

The Story Of The Opera

ACT I

The opera begins at night in the Aliaferia Palace in Saragossa, home of the Princess of Aragon. We are outside the apartments of the Count di Luna who commands the troops loyal to the Princess in her war with the rebel Prince of Urgel.

Ferrando, di Luna's chief lieutenant, rouses the Count's troops who are drowsily lying about. He warns them to keep a good watch for di Luna's safety, for the Count is spending another night under the balcony of the woman he loves. The Count has a rival—an unknown troubadour—for his beloved's affection, and he is tormented by jealousy.

The soldiers ask Ferrando to tell them the story of the Count's brother, Garzia, who had disappeared in infancy. He tells them that one day an old hag was discovered near the child's cradle. Servants drove her away, but the child grew sick and his father was sure the woman had cast a spell on his son. She was captured and burned alive for witchcraft, and Garzia disappeared. It was assumed that the witch's daughter had stolen the baby, and the next day the remains of a child's body were found on a still-smoking fire.

The Count would not accept that his son was dead; he was sure the woman who snatched Garzia still had him. Though he spent the rest of his life searching for her, his efforts were in vain. On his deathbed, he made his remaining son promise to continue the hunt. Ferrando says that although it has been 20 years, he would recognize the witch's daughter, who is believed to haunt the castle still, and to have killed retainers of the Count. Suddenly the clock strikes midnight, and the men retreat in terror.

Next we are in the palace gardens where Leonora, lady-in-waiting to the Princess, is strolling with her friend Ines. Lenora tells Ines how she fell in love with an unknown knight who had won a tournament. The civil war started not long after, and she lost track of him, until one night she heard a troubadour singing in the palace garden. When he mentioned her name in his song, she ran to the window where she saw and recognized him. Ines warns her of the dangers of loving this unknown man but Leonora says that her love for the troubadour is eternal. They go to their rooms and the Count, who has noticed the light on in Leonora's window, begins to enter the palace. He stops when, to his fury, he hears the troubadour's voice coming nearer. Just as the singer arrives, Leonora reappears; in the darkness she confuses the Count di Luna for his rival and rushes into his arms. "Faithless one!" shouts the troubadour when he sees this, but Leonora realizes her error and her excuses are quickly accepted. The Count challenges him to a duel, and the troubadour identifies himself as Manrico. Di Luna recognizes that name as one of Urgel's captains, and the rivalry takes on even greater meaning: They are opponents in love as well as in war. The scene ends with both men leaving to fight their duel.

ACT II

Weeks later, we are in the mountains of Biscay. A company of gypsies is waking up and greeting the dawn with a rousing chorus, to which they beat time on their anvils. In their midst, by the fire, sits Azucena, an old gypsy woman, with Manrico by her side. Seemingly entranced by the fire, she is singing her own song full of weird, terrifying images—savage flames, an exultant crowd and an old woman beaten and dragged by soldiers to the fire, crying, "Avenge me! Avenge me!" As Azucena finishes her song the gypsies depart to begin their day's work, but Manrico stays behind and asks his "mother" to explain her song. She tells how, holding her own child, she witnessed her mother being burned at the stake. Her mother tried to get a parting mother's blessing to Azucena and the child, but the soldiers pushed her away and thrust the old woman into the flames. From the billowing flames her mother's final words were a plea to Azucena to avenge her. Fulfilling her mother's last request, she went to Count di Luna's palace and kidnapped his son. Her intention was to throw the child onto a pyre just as her mother had been, but the baby's cries were so moving that she wavered at the last moment. Her mother's ghost appeared just then demanding vengeance, and Azucena, terrified and delirious, grabbed the baby and hurled it into the fire. When she recovered from her delirium, she realized that in her panic she had grabbed the wrong baby: She had killed her own child instead of the Count's.

Manrico, by now horrified and confused, asks Azucena if he is, then, not really her son. Azucena hastily and anxiously assures him that she is his mother, and points out that she had, after all, recently gone to the battlefield at Pelilla and nursed him back to health after he'd been left for dead. Manrico recounts the battle in which he stood alone against the Count di Luna, and how later, in a duel, he could have killed him. He notes that it was strange, but just as he was going to finish off his rival, a voice from above held him back. Azucena makes him promise not to hold back his sword if he ever again has the Count at his disposal.

A messenger appears with orders from Prince of Urgel. The fortress of Castellor has been captured, and he orders Manrico to take command of it. The messenger also tells Manrico that Leonora, thinking him dead in the Battle of Pelilla, is about to join a convent. Despite Azucena's frantic attempt to convince him that his wounds have not healed enough for him to leave so soon, Manrico rushes to take his command and to stop Leonora from taking the veil.

The Count, meanwhile, has also decided to prevent Leonora from becoming a nun. Now that his rival is dead (or so he believes), he will not lose her. He plans to carry her off before she enters the convent. He gathers his followers at the nunnery, not far from Castellor, and awaits Leonora's arrival. When di Luna hears the bell announcing the beginning of the ceremony, in his impassioned madness he declares that not even God will take her from him. Leonora, escorted by Ines, appears and di Luna and his men attempt to take her; however, Manrico arrives just in time. Leonora is overjoyed and the Count is astonished. Before di Luna can order his men to take them, Ruiz, Manrico's lieutenant, arrives with a larger force of troops and the Count is forced to retreat.

ACT III

Manrico has taken command of Castellor, and di Luna is laying siege to the fortress. Ferrando rouses the Count's troops with promises of the riches they will receive once they have taken the stronghold. Di Luna broods over his dilemma: His rival is alive and about to marry Leonora in Castellor. Ferrando enters, dragging Azucena with him; she has been captured wandering around their camp. The Count interrogates her and she tells him she is looking for her son. Ferrando recognizes her as the daughter of the old witch, the murderer of di Luna's brother. When he tells the Count this, Azucena cries out in desperation for "her son, Manrico" to save her. Once again fortune appears to bless di Luna; the thought that he has an opportunity to deal a savage blow to Manrico, to prevent him marrying Leonora, makes him ecstatic. He announces that Azucena will suffer the same fate as her mother, and orders her imprisoned.

Inside Castellor, Manrico and Leonora are about to be married. She is afraid of the Count's besieging forces, but Manrico reassures her that love has given him all the strength and courage he will need. Even if he should die in the ensuing battle, they will be united again as husband and wife in heaven. The couple are singing of their love when Ruiz enters, bringing word of Azucena's capture and announced execution. Manrico immediately gathers his men and prepares to rescue his mother from the pyre.

ACT IV

Castellor falls to di Luna, and Manrico's attempt to rescue his mother fails; mother and son are now imprisoned in the same cell high in a tower. In the garden below, Leonora sings of her love for Manrico as she hears the distant sound of monks chanting for the souls of those about to die. Manrico joins in, exclaiming his own eternal love for Leonora.

Determined to save Manrico, Leonora concocts a plan to free him, even if it means sacrificing her own life, and departs. Di Luna enters, contemplating the fate of Manrico and Azucena. His satisfaction is not complete, however, because in the siege he lost track of Leonora. Leonora suddenly enters and begins bargaining with the Count for Manrico's life; she offers herself in return for Manrico's freedom. Di Luna joyfully accepts this desperate deal, but when he turns away for a moment, Leonora swallows a vial of poison she had secreted in a ring, singing, "You'll have me, but I'll be a cold and lifeless corpse."

The final scene takes place in the tower cell, where Manrico and Azucena await execution. Terrified by distressing nightmares, Azucena is frantic. Manrico soothes her to sleep with memories of their mountain home. Leonora enters, announcing that she has procured his release and begs him to flee, but he asks how she managed to free him. When Leonora fails to answer, Manrico realizes the truth. Shocked by her faithlessness, he curses her. The poison now begins to take effect and Leonora confesses to the deal she made with di Luna. As the Count enters the cell, Leonora is dying in Manrico's arms and di Luna, witnessing his love once again being torn from his grip, orders Manrico taken away and executed immediately. Azucena awakens from her fitful sleep and the Count pulls her to the window to watch her son's death. As the axe falls, Azucena yells wildly that di Luna has just had his own brother executed. "Mother, you are avenged!" she exclaims. The Count, horrified, cries in despair, "And I still live!" as the curtain falls.

Il Trovatore

GIUSEPPE VERDI (1813-1901)

Leonora..Leontyne Price
Azucena...Elena Obraztsova
Manrico...Franco Bonisolli
Count di Luna...Piero Cappuccilli
Ferrando..Ruggero Raimondi

Conducted by Herbert von Karajan
Berlin Philharmonic

The Artists

LEONTYNE PRICE (Leonora)

Leontyne Price was born in Laurel, Mississippi in 1927, where she later took piano and singing instruction and performed in local concerts. In 1948 she received her B. A. and was awarded a scholarship at the Julliard School of Music in New York. There she received vocal taining from Florence Page Kimball and also joined the Opera Workshop under the direction of Frederic Cohen. Virgil Thomson heard her perform the role of Mistress Ford in *Falstaff* and invited her to sing in the revival of his opera *4 Saints in 3 Acts* in 1952. Soon after, she performed the role of Bess in Gershwin's *Porgy and Bess* on a tour of the U.S. (1952-54) and in Europe (1955). Her televised 1955 performance of Tosca created a sensation both artistically and politically, as Price was the first African-American to take up the role of the Italian diva. Her remarkable talents soon assured her fame. In 1957 she made her debut in San Francisco as Aïda, a role which proved eminently harmonious with her passionate artistry. Price also sang Aïda with the Vienna State Opera in 1958 under the direction of Herbert von Karajan and at Covent Garden in London. It was as Aïda, in 1959, that she became the first African-American woman to sing with La Scala.

In January, 1961 Price made her first appearance at the Metropolitan Opera in New York as Leonora in *Il trovatore*. Over the next decade she gave a series of

highly successful performances at the Metropolitan: Aïda, Madame Butterfly and Donna Anna, 1961; Tosca, 1962; Pamina, 1964 and in 1966 Cleopatra, in the premiere of Samuel Barber's opera *Antony and Cleopatra*, at the opening of the new Metropolitan Opera House at Lincoln Center. In the 1970s Price continued to be a key diva at the Met, singing Madame Butterfly again in 1973, the title role of *Manon Lescaut* in 1975 and Aïda in 1976, which she repeated for her farewell performance to the operatic stage in a televised production broadcast live on January 3, 1985. Her big, glorious sound has been likened as frequently to an oil gusher as a pillar of silver; in her prime she was an ideal Verdi soprano.

ELENA OBRAZTSOVA (Azucena)

This outstanding Russian mezzo-soprano was born in Leningrad on July 7, 1937. She graduated from the Leningrad Conservatory in 1964 after making her operatic debut in *Boris Godunov* at Moscow's Bolshoi Theater in 1963. Her first U.S. tour was with the Bolshoi troop in 1975, and she made her debut at the Metropolitan Opera House singing Amneris in Verdi's *Aïda*. After an absence of almost ten years, she appeared in a 1987 New York recital, and was invited back to the Met. Named a National Artist of the RSFSR in 1973, she received the Lenin Prize three years later. These honors in her native land reflect her remarkable theatricality, her huge pliable voice and the potency of her characterizations. She has sung most of the mezzo roles in the Russian operatic repertoire, as well as such standard roles as Carmen, Eboli, Dalila and of course, Azucena.

FRANCO BONISOLLI (Manrico)

Tenor Franco Bonisolli was born in Rovereto, Italy in 1937 and made his professional debut in 1962 at the Spoleto Festival as Ruggero in Puccini's *La rondine*. Alfredo

in *La traviata* was his debut role at both the Vienna Staatsoper and the San Francisco Opera in 1968 and 1969 respectively. While he was making a name for himself in the operas of Verdi and the verismo composers, he debuted at the Metropolitan Opera in the *bel canto* part of Count Almaviva in Rossini's *Il barbiere di Siviglia*. Throughout his career he has alternated between heavy and light roles, singing the tenor leads in *Turandot, La donna del lago, Aïda, La gioconda, Carmen* and many other works. Known for his stentorian high notes, Bonisolli has been criticized for his lack of sensitivity, while being praised—invariably at the same time—for the excitement he usually brings to each role he sings.

Piero Cappuccilli (Count di Luna)
Since his debut at the Teatro Nuovo in Milan in 1957, Italian native Piero Cappuccilli has appeared internationally. His 1960 Metropolitan Opera debut in New York was in *La traviata* as Germont; the same year he recorded the role of Enrico Ashton in Donizetti's *Lucia di Lammermoor* with Maria Callas. His La Scala debut in 1964 (also as Enrico) was a great success and he quickly became a house

FRANCO BONISOLLI IN A SAN FRANCISCO OPERA PRODUCTION OF TROVATORE, 1986

favorite. Cappuccilli debuted at London's Covent Garden in 1967 (again as Germont) and at the age of 60 triumphed there singing in both *Cavalleria Rusticana* and *I Pagliacci* in the same evening. Though he was known throughout most of his career more for his large, healthy sound than for his finesse, the late 1970s found Cappuccilli growing in sensitivity and elegance while maintaining both his power and remarkable breath control.

RUGGERO RAIMONDI (Ferrando)
An Italian bass born in Bologna in 1941, Ruggero Raimondi was educated at the Accademia di Santa Cecilia in Rome. After making his debut as Colline in *Spoleto* in 1964, Raimondi sang at Milan's La Scala beginning in 1967. His Metropolitan Opera debut was as Don Ruy Gomez de Silva in *Ernani* on September 14, 1970. Other noteworthy appearances were at the Paris Opéra, the Bavarian State Opera in Munich and the Deutsche Opera in Berlin. His Don Giovanni was quite distinguished, as was his dramatic rendition of Boris Godunov, for which he gained significant praise. The role of Ferrando suits his even bass voice excellently, although it is far too insignificant a part for him to have sung after the early days of his career for any conductor other than von Karajan.

HERBERT VON KARAJAN (Conductor, Berlin Philharmonic)
When he died near Salzburg, Austria in 1989, Herbert von Karajan was the world's preeminent conductor in the grand Germanic tradition. The path to that vaunted position began in Salzburg in 1908, where he was born into a family of talented musicians. His musical education began at the Salzburg Mozarteum; later in Vienna he attended a technical college and took private piano lessons, then entered the Vienna Academy of Music as a conducting student of Clemens Krauss

RUGGERO RAIMONDI, 1980

and Alexander Wunderer. On December 17, 1928, von Karajan made his conducting debut with a student orchestra at the Academy, and one month later his professional conducting debut with the Salzburg Orchestra; from there he was engaged as conductor of the Ulm Stadttheater (1929-34). In 1933 he joined the Nazi party, and although he was officially de-Nazified by the Allied army of occupation in 1947, his enthusiasm for fascism would haunt him the rest of his life.

In 1934 von Karajan left Ulm for Aachen, where he was made conductor of the Stadttheater and subsequently served as Generalmusikdirektor until 1942. 1938 was an important year in his career: He conducted his first performance with the Berlin Philharmonic, the orchestra with which he became most identified, and led *Fidelio* with the Berlin Staatsoper Orchestra. Notably, he conducted all his scores from memory, including the entire *Ring des Nibelungen.* His fame in Germany led to engagements elsewhere in Europe, and by the end of 1938 von Karajan had conducted opera at La Scala and in

HERBERT VON KARAJAN AT HOME

Belgium, the Netherlands and Scandinavia. In 1939 he was made conductor of the symphony concerts of the Berlin Staatsoper.

Von Karajan began a close 10-year relationship with the Vienna Symphony Orchestra in 1948, but his conducting at the Philharmonic Orchestra of London from 1948 to 1954 did more than anything else to reestablish his career after World War II. When Wilhelm Furtwängler, conductor of the Berlin Philharmonic, died in 1954, von Karajan was chosen to lead the orchestra on its first tour of the United States. Protesters appalled by his Nazi past were on hand for the performance at Carnegie Hall in New York, but this did not stop the musicians from electing him their conductor during their visit to Pittsburgh.

After 1955, von Karajan came to dominate classical music in Europe as no other conductor ever had. Besides holding his permanent position in Berlin, he served as artistic director of the Vienna Staatsoper from 1957 until he resigned in a bitter dispute with its general manager in 1964. He also served as the artistic director of the Salzburg festival during the 1960s. From 1969 to 1971 he held the title of artistic adviser of the Paris Orchestra. In 1967 he organized his own Salzburg Easter Festival, which became one of the world's leading musical events. That same year he was also named conductor-for-life of the Berlin Philharmonic, and finally made his Metropolitan Opera debut conducting *Die Walküre*.

In the 1970s and 1980s von Karajan took the Berlin Philharmonic on frequent tours of Europe, Japan, the Soviet Union and China. He celebrated his 30th anniversary as conductor of the orchestra in 1985, and in 1988 his 60th anniversary as a conductor. In 1987 he led the New Year's Day Concert of the Vienna Philharmonic, televised to millions around the world. Von Karajan made his final appearance in America conducting the Vienna Philharmonic at Carnegie Hall, and retired from the pit within the next year.

The Libretto

Act 1

SCENE ONE

disc no. 1/track 1 A hall in the Aliaferia palace; a door on one side leads into the Count di Luna's apartments. Ferrando and a number of the Count's retainers are resting near the door; some soldiers are pacing back and forth in the background.

FERRANDO
All'erta! All'erta! Il Conte
n'è d'uopo attendere vigilando,
ed egli talor presso i veroni
della sua casa, intere passa le notti.

UOMINI
Gelosia le fiere serpi
gli avventa in petto.

FERRANDO
Nel Trovator, che dai giardini
muove notturno il canto,
d'un rivale a dritto ei teme.

UOMINI
Dalle gravi palpebre
il sonno a discacciar,
la vera storia ci narra
di Garzia, germano al nostro Conte.

FERRANDO
La dirò, venite intorno a me.

FERRANDO
Look sharp there! The Count
must be served with vigilance;
sometimes, near the house of his beloved,
he spends whole nights.

MEN
Jealousy's fierce serpents
are writhing in his breast.

FERRANDO
In the Troubadour, whose song
rises at night from the gardens,
he rightly fears a rival.

MEN
To drive off the sleep
that hangs heavy on our eyelids,
tell us the real story
of Garzia, our Count's brother.

FERRANDO
I'll tell you; gather around me.

ALTRI
Noi pure...Udite, udite.

OTHERS
We, too...Listen then.

disc no. 1/track 2

FERRANDO
Di due figli vivea padre beato,
il buon Conte di Luna.
Fida nutrice del secondo nato
dormia presso la cuna.
Sul romper dell'aurora un bel mattino,
ella dischiude i rai
e chi trova d'accanto a quel bambino?

FERRANDO
There lived a happy father of two sons,
the good Count di Luna.
The second boy's faithful nurse
slept next to his cradle.
As dawn was breaking one fine morning,
she opened her eyes and whom did she find
next to that baby?

UOMINI
Chi? favella... Chi? chi mai?

MEN
Who? Speak...Who was it?

disc no. 1/
tracks 3-5

The fact that the Count's deputy is telling stories and that all of his men are
frightened is hardly the issue here; what is important is that we learn the background to the story in a quick, entertaining fashion. Ferrando's jittery vocal line
draws attention to itself and the "spookiness" of the tale; indeed, at the end,
when he recounts how one of the Count's servants died of fright when the
gypsy appeared to him "at midnight," the clock in real time strikes midnight and
scares the daylights out of Ferrando, the men and us. It may be a cheap trick,
but it gets our attention.

FERRANDO
Abbietta zingara, fosca vegliarda!
Cingeva i simboli di maliarda!
E sul fanciullo, con viso arcigno,
l'occhio affiggeva torvo, sanguigno!
D'orror compresa è la nutrice;
acuto un grido all'aura scioglie;
ed ecco, in meno che labbro il dice
i servi accorrono in quelle soglie;
e fra minacce, urli, percosse
la rea discacciano ch'entrarvi osò.

FERRANDO
A dark, despicable gypsy crone!
Wearing the symbols of a sorceress!
And with a sullen face, over the boy
she cast her bloody, baleful eye!
The nurse is seized with horror;
she utters a sharp cry in the still air;
and, in less time than it takes to tell,
the servants hasten into the room;
and with shouts, blows, threats,
they expel the wretch who dared enter.

UOMINI
Giusto quei petti sdegno commosse;
l'infame vecchia lo provocò!

FERRANDO
Asserì che tirar del fanciullino
l'oroscopo volea. Bugiarda!
Lenta febbre del meschino
la salute struggea!
Coverto di pallor, languido,
affranto, ei tremava la sera,
e il dì traeva in lamentevol pianto:
ammaliato egl'era!
La fattucchiera perseguitata,
fu presa e al rogo fu condannata:
ma rimanea la maledetta
figlia, ministra di ria vendetta!
Compì quest'empia nefando eccesso!
Sparve il fanciullo,
e si rinvenne mal spenta brace
nel sito istesso
ov'arsa un giorno la strega venne!
E d'un bambino, ahimè l'ossame
bruciato a mezzo, fumante ancor!

UOMINI
Ah scellerata! Oh donna infame!
Del par m'investe ira ed orror!
E il padre?

FERRANDO
Brevi e tristi giorni visse;
pur ignoto del cor presentimento
gli diceva che spento
non era il figlio; ed a morir vicino
bramò che il signor nostro
a lui giurasse di non cessar
le indagini. Ah! fur vane!

MEN
Their hearts were moved by righteous scorn;
the crazy crone provoked it!

FERRANDO
She claimed that she wanted to cast
the boy's horoscope. The liar!
A slow fever began to destroy
the poor child's health!
Weak, covered with a strange pallor,
broken, he trembled at night,
and moaned piteously all day long;
he was bewitched!
The witch was pursued,
seized and condemned to the stake;
but her cursed daughter was left,
to administer a horrible revenge!
This criminal committed an unspeakable act!
The child disappeared,
and they found still glowing embers,
on the very same spot
where the witch had once been burned!
And, alas, a child's skeleton,
half-burnt, still smoking!

MEN
Ah! the wicked unspeakable woman!
It fills me with both rage and horror!
What about the father?

FERRANDO
His remaining days were few and sad;
yet an undefined presentiment
at heart told him that his son
was not dead; and when he lay dying,
he desired that our master
should swear to him not to stop
his search. Ah! It was in vain!

UOMINI	MEN
E di colei non s'ebbe contezza mai?	And was no news ever had of her?

FERRANDO	FERRANDO
Nulla contezza!	No news!
Oh! dato mi fosse	Oh! were it granted me
rintracciarla un dì!	to track her down some day!

UOMINI	MEN
Ma ravvisarla potresti?	But, could you recognize her?

FERRANDO	FERRANDO
Calcolando gli anni trascorsi, lo potrei.	Considering the years that have passed, I could.

UOMINI	MEN
Sarebbe tempo presso la madre	It would be time to send her
all'inferno spedirla.	to her mother, in hell.

FERRANDO	FERRANDO
All'inferno?	In hell?
È credenza che dimori ancor	It's common belief that
nel mondo l'anima perduta	the wicked witch's damned soul
dell'empia strega, e quando il ciel è nero	still lives in the world, and when the sky
in varie forme altrui si mostri.	is black she shows herself in various shapes.

TUTTI	ALL
È vero! È vero! È vero! È vero!	It's true! It's true!
Sull'orlo dei tetti	On the edge of the rooftops
alcun l'ha veduta!	some people have seen her!
In upupa o strige talora si muta!	Sometimes she changes into a hoopoe or
	an owl!
In corvo tal'altra; più spesso in civetta,	Other times, a raven; more often, a civet-owl,
sull'alba fuggente al par di saetta!	flying through the dawn like an arrow!

FERRANDO	FERRANDO
Morì di paura un servo del Conte	One of the Count's men died of fear
che avea della zingara percossa la fronte!	because he had struck the gypsy's forehead!

57

Morì, morì di paura, morì, morì, morì di paura!

UOMINI
Ah! Ah! Morì! Ah! Ah! Morì!

FERRANDO
Apparve a costui d'un gufo in sembianza,
nell'alta quiete di tacita stanza!

UOMINI
D'un gufo! D'un gufo!

FERRANDO
Con occhi lucenti guardava,
guardava il cielo attristando
d'un urlo feral!

UOMINI
Guardava! Guardava!

FERRANDO
Allor mezzanotte appunto suonava! Ah!

UOMINI
Ah!

(Midnight strikes.)

TUTTI
Ah! Sia maledetta la strega infernal! Ah!

He died, died of fear! He died, died of fear!

MEN
Ah! Ah! He died! Ah! Ah! He died!

FERRANDO
She appeared to him in the form of an owl,
in the deep calm of a silent room!

MEN
Of an owl!

FERRANDO
She looked with gleaming eye,
looked at the sky, sorrowing,
with a bestial cry!

MEN
She looked! She looked!

FERRANDO
Midnight was just striking! Ah!

MEN
Ah!

ALL
Ah! A curse on her the infernal witch! Ah!

(A drum is heard. The soldiers run to the back. The servants gather at the door.)

SCENE TWO

disc no. 1/track 6 The garden of the palace. At the right, a marble stair leads up to the private apartments. Thick clouds conceal the moon. Leonora and Ines are strolling.

INES
Che più t'arresti?
L'ora è tarda; vieni;
di te la regal donna chiese;
l'udisti.

LEONORA
Un'altra notte ancora senza vederlo!

INES
Perigliosa fiamma tu nutri!
Oh come, dove la primiera favilla
in te s'apprese?

LEONORA
Ne' tornei. V'apparve,
bruno le vesti ed il cimier,
lo scudo bruno e di stemma ignudo,
sconosciuto guerrier,
che dell'agone gli onori ottenne.
Al vincitor sul crine il serto io posi.

Civil guerra intanto arse – nol vidi più!
Come d'aurato sogno
fuggente immago! ed era volta
lunga stagion, ma poi...

INES
Che avvenne?

LEONORA
Ascolta!

INES
Why stay here any longer?
It's late; come;
the queen asked about you;
you heard her.

LEONORA
Yet another night without seeing him!

INES
You're nursing a dangerous flame!
Oh how, where did its first spark
strike you?

LEONORA
At the tourney. There appeared,
in black armour and black helmet,
with black shield and without crest,
an unknown warrior,
who won the honours of the arena.
On the victor's head I placed the crown.

Then civil war raged – I saw him no more!
Like the fleeting image
of a golden dream! and a long
time passed, but then...

INES
What happened?

LEONORA
Listen!

Leonora, like Ferrando, has a tale to tell, but where he was full of bluster, she's full of lyricism and yearning - the latter heard in the exquisite rise of her vocal line (00:39, 02:20). When she recounts her happiness - how "the earth seemed like heaven," her voice reaches to the heaven of a D flat above high C - (03:38) a truly beatific sound.

Tacea la notte placida	The serene night was silent
e bella in ciel sereno;	and, lovely in the calm sky,
la luna il viso argenteo	the moon happily revealed
mostrava lieto e pieno!	its silvery and full face!
Quando suonar per l'aere,	When, resounding in the air
infino allor sì muto,	which till then had been so quiet,
dolci s'udiro e flebili	sweet and sad were heard
gli accordi d'un liuto,	the sounds of a lute,
e versi melanconici	and a troubadour
un trovator cantò.	sang some melancholy verses.
Versi di prece ed umile,	Verses, beseeching and humble,
qual d'uom che prega Iddio:	like a man praying to God:
in quella ripeteasi un nome,	and in them was repeated a name,
il nome mio!	my name!
Corsi al veron sollecita...	I ran eagerly to the balcony...
Egli era, egli era desso!	There he was; it was he!
Gioia provai che agl'angeli	I felt a joy that only the angels
solo è provar concesso!	are allowed to feel!
Al cor, al guardo estatico	To my heart, my ecstatic eyes,
la terra un ciel sembrò!	the earth seemed like heaven!
Al cor, ecc.	To my heart, etc.

Disc no. 1/track 8

INES	**INES**
Quanto narrasti di turbamento	What you've told me has filled
m'ha piena l'alma! Io temo...	my soul with anguish! I fear...
LEONORA	**LEONORA**
Invano!	Needlessly...

INES
Dubbio, ma tristo presentimento
in me risvegli quest'uomo arcano!
Tenta obbliarlo.

LEONORA
Che dici? Oh basti!

INES
Cedi al consiglio dell'amistà,
cedi!

LEONORA
Obliarlo! Ah! tu parlasti detto
che intender l'alma non sa.

INES
A sad, but vague presentiment
is stirred in me by this mysterious man!
Try to forget him.

LEONORA
What are you saying? Enough!

INES
Give way to a friend's advice,
do give way!

LEONORA
Forget him! Ah, you've spoken a word
that my soul cannot understand.

disc no. 1/track 9 With plucked cellos and trilling violins and winds Leonora vocally bounces around with great virtuousity, expressing her wild desires, her "intoxication" and her extravagant love for her troubadour.

Di tale amor che dirsi
mal può dalla parola,
d'amor che intendo io sola,
il cor s'inebriò.
Il mio destino compiersi
non può che a lui d'appresso.
S'io non vivrò per esso,
per esso morirò,
s'io non vivrò per esso, ecc.

With such love that words
can scarcely tell,
of a love that only I know,
my heart is intoxicated.
My fate can be fulfilled
only at his side.
If I can't live for him,
then for him I'll die.
If I can't live for him, etc

(They go up to their rooms. Then the Count di Luna comes in.)

disc no. 1/track 10

CONTE
Tace la notte!

COUNT
The night is still!

Immersa nel sonno	The queen is surely
è certo la regal signora:	immersed in sleep;
ma veglia la sua dama –	but her lady is wakeful –
Oh! Leonora, tu desta sei:	Oh! Leonora you're awake;
mel dice da quel verone	I'm told, from that balcony,
tremolante un raggio	by the quivering ray
della notturna lampa.	of your night lamp.
Ah! l'amorosa fiamma	Ah! the flame of love
m'arde ogni fibra!	burns my every fibre!
Ch'io ti vegga è d'uopo,	I must see you,
che tu m'intenda. Vengo.	you must hear me. I'm coming.
A noi supremo è tal momento.	This is our supreme moment.

(He starts to go up the steps, but stops, hearing a lute.)

disc no. 1/track 11 The count's passionate reverie over Leonora is interrupted by—bizarrely enough—the sound of an off-stage harp. It is accompanying Manrico, who sings a simple but elegant "troubadour"-like melody which makes us like him at once—and makes the Count trmble with jealousy.

Il Trovator! Io fremo!	The Troubadour! I tremble with rage!
MANRICO *(fuori scena)*	**MANRICO** *(out of sight)*
Deserto sulla terra,	All alone on the earth,
col rio destin in guerra,	at war with his evil fate,
è sola speme un cor,	his only hope is in one heart,
un cor al Trovator.	a heart for the Troubadour.
CONTE	**COUNT**
Oh detti! Io fremo!	These words! I tremble with rage!
MANRICO	**MANRICO**
Ma s'ei quel cor possiede,	But he possesses that heart,
bello di casta fede,	lovely with its chaste promise,
CONTE	**COUNT**
Oh detti!	These words!

MANRICO
È d'ogni re maggior...

CONTE
Oh gelosia!

MANRICO
È d'ogni re maggior,
maggior il Trovator.

CONTE
Non m'inganno... Ella scende!

(Leonora comes down into the garden and runs towards the Count.)

disc no. 1/track 12

LEONORA
Anima mia!

CONTE
(Che far?)

LEONORA
Più dell'usato è tarda l'ora:
io ne contai gl'istanti
co' palpiti del core!
Alfin ti guida pietoso amor
fra queste braccia.

MANRICO *(ancora fra gli alberi)*
Infida!

(The moon comes out from the clouds and reveals a man whose face is hidden by his visor.)

LEONORA
Qual voce!

MANRICO
He's greater than any king...

COUNT
What jealousy!

MANRICO
He's greater than any king,
greater is the Troubadour.

COUNT
I'm not mistaken...She's coming down!

LEONORA
My dearest!

COUNT
(What shall I do?)

LEONORA
The hour is later than usual:
I counted its instants
by the beating of my heart!
At last, merciful love leads you
to my arms.

MANRICO *(still among the trees)*
Faithless!

LEONORA
That voice!

(Recognizing both of them, Leonora throws herself at Manrico's feet.)

Ah, dalle tenebre tratta in errore io fui!	Ah, the darkness deceived me!
A te credea rivolgere	I thought that I was speaking
l'accento, e non a lui...	to you, not him...
A te, che l'alma mia	To you, that my soul
sol chiede, sol desia.	only wants, desires.
Io t'amo, il giuro, t'amo	I love you, I swear it, love you
d'immenso, eterno amor!	with eternal, immense love!

CONTE
Ed osi!

COUNT
You dare!

MANRICO
Ah, più non bramo!

MANRICO
Ah, I ask no more!

CONTE
Avvampo di furor! Avvampo di furor!

COUNT
I'm burning with fury!

LEONORA
Io t'amo! Io t'amo!

LEONORA
I love you! I love you!

MANRICO
Ah, più non bramo!

MANRICO
Ah, I ask no more!

CONTE
Se un vil non sei, discovriti!

COUNT
If you're not a coward, reveal yourself!

LEONORA
(Ohimè!)

LEONORA
(Alas!)

CONTE
Palesa il nome!

COUNT
Tell me your name!

LEONORA
(Deh, per pietà!)

LEONORA
(Ah, have mercy!)

MANRICO
Ravvisami: Manrico io son!

CONTE
Tu! Come? Insano, temerario!
D'Urgel seguace,
a morte proscritto, ardisci
volgerti a queste regie porte?

MANRICO
Che tardi?
Or via le guardie appella,
ed il rivale al ferro
del carnefice consegna!

CONTE
Il tuo fatale istante
assai più prossimo è,
dissennato! Vieni...

LEONORA
Conte!

CONTE
Al mio sdegno vittima
è d'uopo ch'io ti sveni.

LEONORA
Oh ciel, t'arresta!

CONTE
Seguimi!

MANRICO
Andiam!

MANRICO
Know me then: I'm Manrico!

COUNT
You! What? Mad, foolhardy man!
A follower of Urgel,
sentenced to death, you dare
approach these royal gates?

MANRICO
Why are you delaying?
Come, call the guards,
and hand your rival over
to the executioner's blade!

COUNT
Your last moment
is much nearer,
insane man! Come...

LEONORA
Count!

COUNT
I must have your blood,
victim of my contempt.

LEONORA
Oh heaven, stop!

COUNT
Follow me!

MANRICO
Let's go!

LEONORA
(Che mai farò?)

CONTE
Seguimi!

MANRICO
Andiam!

LEONORA
(Un sol mio grido perdere lo puote!)
M'odi!

CONTE
No!

LEONORA
(What shall I do?)

COUNT
Follow me!

MANRICO
Let's go!

LEONORA
(One cry from me could undo him!)
Hear me out!

COUNT
No!

The act's finale is chock full of nervous energy—all three soloists sing staccato phrases expressing different things, but Manrico and Leonora are mostly together, while the Count offers an argumentative counterpoint.

Di geloso amor sprezzato,
arde in me tremendo il fuoco!
Il tuo sangue, o sciagurato,
ad estinguerlo fia poco!
Dirgli, o folle,
io t'amo, ardisti!
Ei più vivere non può.
Un accento proferisti
che a morir lo condannò!
Un accento proferisti, ecc.

My spurned and jealous love
burns in me with a terrible flame!
Your blood, wretch, would be
hardly enough to put it out!
Foolish girl, you dared
to tell him, "I love you".
He can live no longer.
You uttered a word
that condemned him to die!
You uttered a word, etc.

LEONORA
Un istante almen dia loco
il tuo sdegno alla ragione:
io, sol io di tanto foco
son pur troppo la cagione!
Piombi, piombi il tuo furore

LEONORA
At least for a moment, let your scorn
make room for reasoning:
I, and only I, am unfortunately
the cause of all your fire!
So let your fury, fall

sulla rea che t'oltraggiò,
vibra il ferro in questo core
che te amar non vuol né può.

MANRICO
Del superbo è vana l'ira;
ei cadrà da me trafitto:
il mortal, che amor t'inspira,
dall'amor fu reso invitto.

(to the Count)

La tua sorte è già compita,
l'ora omai per te suonò!
Il suo core e la tua vita
il destino a me serbò!

CONTE
Dirgli, oh folle, ecc.
Il tuo sangue, o sciagurato,
ad estinguerlo fia poco!
Dirgli, o folle,
io t'amo, ardisti!
Ei più vivere non può, ecc.

LEONORA
Piombi, ah! piombi il tuo furore
sulla rea che t'oltraggiò,
vibra il ferro in questo core
che te amar non vuol né può! ecc.

MANRICO
La tua sorte è già compita,
l'ora omai per te suonò!
Il suo core e la tua vita
il destino a me serbò, ecc.

on the evil girl who offended you;
plunge your sword into this heart
that cannot, will not love you.

MANRICO
The haughty man's wrath is in vain;:
He'll fall, run through by me;
the man who can inspire your love
is made by love invaluable.

Your fate is already sealed;
your hour has struck now!
Destiny has given to me
her heart and your life!

COUNT
Foolish girl, you dared, etc
Your blood, wretch, would be
hardly enough to put it out!
Foolish girl, you dared
to tell him "I love you".
He can live no longer, etc.

LEONORA
So let your fury fall, fall
on the evil girl who offended you;
plunge your sword into this heart
that cannot, will not love you! etc.

MANRICO
Your fate is already sealed,
your hour has struck now!
Destiny has given to me
her heart and your life, etc.

CONTE

Ah! di geloso amor sprezzato
arde in me tremendo il foco!
Un accento proferisti
che a morir lo condannò! ecc.

COUNT

Ah! my spurned and jealous love
burns in me with a terrible flame!
You uttered a word
that condemned him to die! etc.

(The two men go off, swords in hand. Leonora falls senseless.)

Act 2

SCENE ONE

disc no. 1/track 14   The slopes of a mountain in Biscay. It is dawn. A great fire is burning. Azucena is sitting by the fire. Manrico is stretched out at her side, wrapped up in his cloak. His helmet lies at his feet, his sword is in his hands, and he is staring at it motionlessly. A band of gypsies is scattered around them.

ZINGARI

Vedi! le fosche notturne spoglie
de' cieli sveste l'immensa vôlta;
sembra una vedova che alfin si toglie
i bruni panni ond'era involta.
All'opra! All'opra! Dàgli! Martella!
Chi del gitano i giorni abbella?
La zingarella!

GYPSIES

See! the heaven's great vault
removes its gloomy, night-time tatters!
It seems like a widow who takes off at last
the dark clothes that enfolded her.
To work! To work! At it! Hammer!
Who brightens the gypsy man's days?
The gypsy maid.

(to the women, pausing in their work)

Versami un tratto: lena e coraggio
il corpo e l'anima traggon dal bere.
Oh, guarda! guarda! Del sole un raggio
brilla più vivido nel mio/tuo bicchiere!

Pour me a draught: strength and courage
the body and soul draw from drinking.
Oh, look, look! A ray of the sun
sparkles brighter in my/your glass!

All'opra! All'opra!
Chi del gitano i giorni abbella?
La zingarella!

To work! To work!
Who brightens the gypsy man's days?
The gypsy maid!

(as Azucena is singing, the gypsies gather around her.)

disc no. 1/track 15 The chronically terrified and jumpy Azucena here introduces herself to us by recounting a horrible event which occurred years ago. The flickering flames are heard in her very first lines, complete with fidgety trills.

AZUCENA
Stride la vampa! La folla indomita
corre a quel foco lieta in sembianza!
Urli di gioia intorno echeggiano:
cinta di sgherri donna s'avanza!
Sinistra splende sui volti orribili
la tetra fiamma che s'alza, che s'alza al ciel!
Stride la vampa! Giunge la vittima
nero vestita, discinta e scalza!
Grido feroce di morte levasi,
l'eco il ripete di balza in balza!
Sinistra splende, ecc.

AZUCENA
The flame crackles! The unrestrained mob
runs to that fire, their faces all happy!
Shouts of joy re-echo around;
Surrounded by killers, a woman comes
forward!
Sinister, shining on the horrible faces,
the ghastly flame rises, rises towards heaven!
The flame crackles! The victim arrives,
dressed in black, dishevelled, barefoot!
A fierce shout of death is raised,
its echo repeated from hill to hill!
Sinister, shining, etc.

disc no. 1/track 16

ZINGARI
Mesta è la tua canzon!

GYPSIES
Your song's a sad one!

AZUCENA
Del pari mesta
che la storia funesta
da cui tragge argomento!
Mi vendica! mi vendica!

AZUCENA
Equally sad
as the terrible story
that inspired it!
Avenge me! Avenge me!

MANRICO
(L'arcana parola ognor!)

MANRICO
(That mysterious phrase again!)

69

UNO ZINGARO
Compagni, avanza il giorno;
a procacciarci un pan,
su! su! scendiamo
per le propinque ville.

ZINGARI
Andiamo! Andiamo!
Chi del gitano i giorni abbella? ecc.

(They go off, singing.)

disc no. 1/track 17

MANRICO
Soli or siamo. Deh, narra
quella storia funesta.

AZUCENA
E tu la ignori, tu pur?
Ma, giovinetto, i passi tuoi
d'ambizion lo sprone lungi traea!
Dell'ava il fine acerbo
è quest'istoria.
La incolpò superbo
Conte di malefizio,
onde asseria côlto un bambin
suo figlio; essa bruciata venne
ov'arde quel foco!

MANRICO
Ahi! sciagurata!

A GYPSY
Companions, day is approaching;
to forage for our daily bread,
come, come, let's go down
to the nearby villages.

GYPSIES
Let's go! Let's go!
Who brightens the gypsy man's days? etc.

MANRICO
We're alone now. Ah, tell me
that terrible story.

AZUCENA
You? Even you don't know it?
But, as a boy, the spur of ambition
drove your steps far from here!
This is the story
of your grandmother's bitter end.
A haughty
Count accused her
of witchcraft, and said that a child, his son,
had been bewitched; she was burned
where that fire gleams!

MANRICO
Ah, the wretch!

disc no. 1/track 18 Now it is time for Azucena (like Ferrando and Leonora) to tell us a story, and this one is hair-raising. It's not as if it surprises us, since it takes over where Ferrando's had left off, but in its short, choppy phrases, we see that Azucena is the opposite of Leonora: Azucena's has nightmares, Leonora has dreams. Even from the opening measures the oboe, with its falling line, seems to be mourning for her, while the strings keep the tension going. With its shifts from quiet to loud and back, and her hallucinations so vivid (02:45) her story is hard to ignore.

AZUCENA
Condotta ell'era in ceppi
al suo destin tremendo;
col figlio sulle braccia,
io la seguia piangendo:
infino ad essa un varco tentai,
ma invano; aprirmi
invan tentò la misera
fermarsi e benedirmi!
Che, fra bestemmie oscene,
pungendola coi ferri,
al rogo la cacciavano
gli scellerati sgherri! –
Allor, con tronco accento,
mi vendica! sclamò.
Quel detto un eco eterno
in questo cor lasciò.

MANRICO
La vendicasti?

AZUCENA
Il figlio giunsi a rapir del Conte;
lo trascinai qui meco –
le fiamme ardean già pronte.

MANRICO
Le fiamme? Oh ciel! Tu forse...?

AZUCENA
She was led in irons
to her terrible fate;
with my baby in my arms
I followed her, weeping;
I tried to make my way
to her, but in vain;
and in vain the poor woman
tried to stop and bless me!
Then, amid obscene curses,
pricking her with their swords,
they forced her to the stake,
those horrible killers! –
Then, in a broken voice,
"Avenge me", she cried.
Those words left in my heart
an eternal echo.

MANRICO
Did you avenge her?

AZUCENA
I managed to steal the Count's son;
I dragged him here with me –
the flames were ready, burning.

MANRICO
The flames? Oh heaven! Did you...?

AZUCENA

Ei distruggeasi in pianto,
io mi sentiva il cor dilaniato, infranto!
Quand'ecco agl'egri spirti,
come in un sogno, apparve
la vision ferale di spaventose larve!
Gli sgherri! ed il supplizio!
La madre smorta in volto,
scalza, discinta!
Il grido! il grido!
Il noto grido ascolto!
"Mi vendica!"
La mano convulsa stendo...
stringo la vittima,
nel foco la traggo, la sospingo!
Cessa il fatal delirio,
l'orrida scena fugge,
la fiamma sol divampa,
e la sua preda strugge!
Pur volgo intorno il guardo
e innanzi a me vegg'io
dell'empio Conte il figlio!

MANRICO
Ah! che dici?

AZUCENA
Il figlio mio, mio figlio avea bruciato!

MANRICO
Ah! Qual orror!

AZUCENA
Ah! Mio figlio! Mio figlio!
Il figlio mio avea bruciato!

MANRICO
Quale orror! Ah! quale orror!

AZUCENA

He was racked with sobs;
I felt my heart, torn, broken!
When, lo, to my weak spirits,
as in a dream, appeared
the bestial vision of frightful forms!
The killers! and the torture!
My mother with blanched face,
dishevelled barefoot!
Her cry! Her cry!
I hear the familiar cry!
"Avenge me!"
I stretch out my shaking hand...
seize the victim,
draw him to the fire, and push!
The fatal madness ends,
the horrible scene disappears;
only the flame rages,
and destroys its prey!
And yet, I look around
and before me I see
the wicked Count's son!

MANRICO
Ah! what are you saying?

AZUCENA
I had burned my own, my own son!

MANRICO
Ah! How horrible!

AZUCENA
Ah! My son! My son!
I had burned my own son!

MANRICO
How terrible! Ah! how horrible!

AZUCENA
Sul capo mio le chiome
sento drizzarsi ancor!

disc no. 1/track 19

MANRICO
Non son tuo figlio!
E chi son io? Chi dunque?

AZUCENA
Tu sei mio figlio!

MANRICO
Eppur dicesti...

AZUCENA
Ah forse? che vuoi?
Quando al pensier s'affaccia
il truce caso
lo spirto intenebrato pone
stolte parole sul mio labbro.
Madre, tenera madre
non m'avesti ognora?

MANRICO
Potrei negarlo?

AZUCENA
A me, se vivi ancora,
nol dêi?
Notturna, nei pugnati campi
di Pelilla, ove spento fama
ti disse, a darti sepoltura
non mossi?
La fuggente aura vital

AZUCENA
I can still feel the hair
stand up on my head!

MANRICO
I'm not your son!
Who am I? Who, then?

AZUCENA
You are my son!

MANRICO
Yet you said...

AZUCENA
Perhaps I did. You know how it is...
When the ghastly event
comes into my mind
my clouded spirit sets
foolish words on my lips.
Haven't I always been a mother,
a tender mother to you?

MANRICO
Can I deny it?

AZUCENA
If you're still alive,
don't you owe it to me?
At night, over the battlefields
of Pelilla, where the report went
that you were dead, didn't I come
to give you burial?
Didn't I discover your fleeting

non iscovrì? Nel seno
non l'arrestò materno affetto?
E quante cure non spesi
a risanar le tante ferite!

MANRICO
Che portai nel dì fatale,
ma tutte qui, nel petto!
Io sol, fra mille già sbandati,
al nemico volgendo ancor la faccia!
Il rio Di Luna su me piombò
col suo drappello: io caddi!
Però da forte io caddi!

AZUCENA
Ecco mercede ai giorni
che l'infame nel singolar certame
ebbe salvi da te!
Qual t'acciecava strana pietà per esso?

MANRICO
Oh madre! Non saprei dirlo a me stesso!

AZUCENA
Strana pietà! Strana pietà!

disc no 1/track 20

MANRICO
Mal reggendo all'aspro assalto,
ei già tocco il suolo avea:
balenava il colpo in alto
che trafiggerlo dovea.
Quando arresta un moto arcano
nel discender questa mano!
Le mie fibre acuto gelo

breath of life? And didn't maternal
love hold it in your breast?
And what care I showed
to heal all those wounds!

MANRICO
That I bore on that fatal day!
But all of them, here, in my chest!
Only I, among the retreating thousand,
turned my face still towards the foe!
The evil Di Luna fell upon me
with his escort: I fell!
But I fell like a strong man!

AZUCENA
That was the thanks for his life,
which in that odd duel,
the monster was given, by you!
Ah, what strange pity for him blinded you?

MANRICO
Oh mother, I can't explain it to myself!

AZUCENA
A strange pity! Strange pity!

MANRICO
Fighting off poorly my fierce attack,
he had already fallen to the ground:
the thrust that was to pierce him
already flashed in the air,
when a mysterious feeling
stopped my hand, as it descended!
Suddenly a sharp chill

fa repente abbrividir!
mentre un grido vien dal cielo,
che mi dice: non ferir.

AZUCENA
Ma nell'alma dell'ingrato
non parlò del ciel un detto!
Oh! se ancor ti spinge il fato
a pugnar col maledetto,
compi, o figlio, qual d'un Dio,
compi allora il cenno mio!
Sino all'elsa questa lama
vibri, immergi al'empio in cor!
Sino all'elsa questa lama, ecc.

MANRICO
Sì, lo giuro, questa lama
scenderà dell'empio in cor! ecc.

(A horn is heard.)

disc no. 1/track 21

L'usato messo Ruiz invia!
Forse...

(He replies with the horn that he carries.)

AZUCENA
"Mi vendica!"

(The messenger enters.)

MANRICO
Inoltra il piè.
Guerresco evento, dimmi, seguia?

ran shuddering through my being
as a cry came down from heaven,
that said to me: Don't strike!

AZUCENA
But to that ingrate's spirit
heaven said not a word!
Ah, if fate should drive you
to fight with that wretch again,
then follow, my son, like a God,
follow then what I tell you to do:
Strike, plunge up to its hilt
that blade in the wicked man's heart!
Strike, plunge up to its hilt, etc.

MANRICO
Yes, I swear it, this blade
will plunge into that wicked heart! etc.

AZUCENA
"Avenge me!"

MANRICO
Come in. Tell me:
did more fighting follow?

MESSO
Risponda il foglio che reco a te.

MANRICO (*Legge.*)
"In nostra possa è Castellor;
ne dêi tu, per cenno del prence,
vigilar le difese.
Ove ti è dato, affrettati a venir.
Giunta la sera, tratta in inganno
di tua morte al grido,
nel vicin chiostro della Croce
il velo cingerà Leonora."
Oh, giusto cielo!

AZUCENA
Che fia?

MANRICO (*al messo*)
Veloce scendi la balza,
ed un cavallo a me provvedi.

MESSO
Corro.

AZUCENA
Manrico!

MANRICO (*al messo*)
Il tempo incalza!
Vola! M'aspetta del colle ai piedi.

(*The messenger hurries off.*)

AZUCENA
E speri? e vuoi?

MESSENGER
Let this letter I bear you give the answer.

MANRICO (*He reads.*)
"Castellor is in our hands;
the Prince's orders are that you
shall supervise its defence.
When you receive this, hurry here.
This evening, deceived by the cry
of your death,
in the nearby Holy Cross Convent,
Leonora will take the veil."
Oh, merciful heaven!

AZUCENA
What is it?

MANRICO (*to the messenger*)
Hurry down the hill,
and prepare a horse for me.

MESSENGER
I'll run.

AZUCENA
Manrico!

MANRICO (*to the messenger*)
Time presses!
Fly! Wait for me at the foot of the hill.

AZUCENA
What do you want of hope to do?

MANRICO
(Perderla! Oh ambascia!
Perder quell'angel!)

AZUCENA
(È fuor di sé!)

MANRICO *(Prende l'elmo e il mantello.)*
Addio!

AZUCENA
No, ferma, odi...

MANRICO
Mi lascia!

AZUCENA
Ferma! Son io che parlo a te!

MANRICO
(To lose her! Oh, woe!
To lose that angel!)

AZUCENA
(He's beside himself.)

MANRICO *(takes his helmet and cloak.)*
Farewell!

AZUCENA
No, stop, hear me...

MANRICO
Let me go!

AZUCENA
Stop! I'm the one who's speaking to you!

disc no. 1/track 22   As Manrico is about to leave to find Leonora, Azucena's motherly love takes over.
She urges him in a quick, urgent line to stay and heal, he counters with his own
passionate feelings. They bid a manic farewell to one-another as the scene ends.

Perigliarti ancor languente
per cammin selvaggio ed ermo!
Le ferite vuoi, demente,
riaprir del petto infermo!
No, soffrirlo non poss'io,
il tuo sangue è sangue mio!
Ogni stilla che ne versi
tu la spremi dal mio cor! Ah! ecc.

To risk yourself, still sickly,
over a wild and steep road!
Mad boy, you mean to re-open
the wounds in your unhealed breast!
No, I cannot bear it:
your blood is my blood!
Every drop you shed of it,
you're pressing from my heart!

MANRICO
Un momento può involarmi
il mio ben, la mia speranza!
No, che basti ad arrestarmi,
terra e ciel non han possanza.

MANRICO
A moment can steal from me
my love, my hope!
No, heaven and earth haven't
the strength to stop me.

AZUCENA
Demente!

MANRICO
Ah! mi sgombra, o madre, i passi,
guai per te, s'io qui restassi!
Tu vedresti a' piedi tuoi
spento il figlio di dolor!

AZUCENA
No, soffrirlo non poss'io...

MANRICO
Guai per te, s'io qui restassi!

AZUCENA
No, soffrirlo non poss'io,
il tuo sangue è sangue mio!
Ogni stilla che ne versi
tu la spremi dal mio cor!

MANRICO
Tu vedresti a' piedi tuoi,
spento il figlio di dolore!
Tu vedresti a' piedi tuoi
spento il figlio di dolor!

AZUCENA
Ferma! ferma!

MANRICO
Mi lascia, mi lascia!

AZUCENA
M'odi, deh! m'odi!

AZUCENA
Madman!

MANRICO
Ah, mother, get out of my way!
Woe to you, should I remain here!
You would see, at your feet,
your son, dead of grief!

AZUCENA
No, I cannot bear it...

MANRICO
Woe to you, should I remain here!

AZUCENA
No, I cannot bear it,
your blood is my blood!
Every drop you shed of it
you're pressing from my heart!

MANRICO
You would see, at your feet,
your son, dead of grief!
You would see, at your feet,
your son, dead of grief!

AZUCENA
Stop! Stop!

MANRICO
Let me go! Let me go!

AZUCENA
Hear me, ah! hear me!

MANRICO
Perder quell'angelo!
Mi lascia, mi lascia, addio! ecc.

AZUCENA
Ah! ferma, m'odi,
son io che parlo a te! ecc.

(He leaves)

MANRICO
To lose that angel!
Let me go! Let me go, farewell! etc.

AZUCENA
Ah! Stop, hear me,
I'm the one who's speaking to you! etc.

SCENE TWO

disc no. 1/track 23 The cloister of a convent in the neighborhood of Castellor. Night. The Count, Ferrando and a few retainers enter cautiously, wrapped in their cloaks.

CONTE
Tutto è deserto
né per l'aure ancora
suona l'usato carme.
In tempo io giungo!

FERRANDO
Ardita opra, o signore, imprendi.

CONTE
Ardita, e qual furente amore
ed irritato orgoglio chiesero a me.
Spento il rival, caduto
ogni ostacol sembrava a' miei desiri;
novello e più possente
ella ne appresta: l'altare!
Ah no! Non fia d'altri Leonora!

COUNT
All is deserted;
nor has the usual hymn
resounded yet on the air.
I've come in time!

FERRANDO
O master, you are undertaking a bold
errand.

COUNT
Bold, yes, it's what furious love
and provoked pride demand of me.
My rival killed, every obstacle
to my wishes seemed to have fallen;
now she prepares a new
and more powerful one; the altar!
Ah no, Leonora shall not belong to others!

For a villain (and one with a potent high G with which he speaks Leonora's name at the close of the recitative in the previous tack), di Luna sure can melt the heart with his elegant, aristocratic melody, one just as classy as Leonora's "Tacea la notte" in Act I, scene 2. Throughout, plush, low strings and woodwinds paint his dreamlike mood.

Leonora è mia!
Il balen del suo sorriso
d'una stella vince il raggio!
Il fulgor del suo bel viso
novo infonde a me coraggio.
Ah! l'amor, l'amore ond'ardo
le favelli in mio favor!
Sperda il sol d'un suo sguardo
la tempesta del mio cor.
Ah! l'amor, l'amore ond'ardo ecc.
(Si sente una campana.)
Qual suono! Oh ciel!

FERRANDO
La squilla vicino il rito annunzia.

CONTE
Ah! pria che giunga all'altar,
si rapisca!

FERRANDO
Oh bada!

CONTE
Taci! Non odo!
Andate.
Di quei faggi all'ombra
celatevi.
Ah! fra poco mia diverrà;
tutto m'investe un foco!

Leonora is mine!
The flashing of her smile
is brighter than a star's ray!
The splendour of her fair face
instills new courage in me.
Ah, let the love that inflames me
speak to her in my favour!
Let the sun of her glance
dispel the storm in my heart.
Ah, let the love that inflames me, etc.
(A bell is heard.)
That sound! Oh heaven!

FERRANDO
Its tolling announces the approaching rite.

COUNT
Ah, before she reaches the altar,
she shall be seized!

FERRANDO
Take care!

COUNT
Silence! I hear nothing!
Go,
and in the shade of those beeches,
conceal yourselves.
Ah, soon she'll become mine;
a fire rages through me!

FERRANDO e SEGUACI
Ardir! andiam, celiamoci fra l'ombre,
nel mister! Ardir! Andiam!
Silenzio! Si compia il suo voler!

FERRANDO AND RETAINERS
Courage! Let's go, and hide in the shadows,
in mystery! Courage! let's go!
Silence! His bidding be done!

disc no. 1/track 26 But just in case we've lost sight of how dangerous he can be, we now find di
Luna singing at the top of his range, with violins jabbing and his vocal line crazi-
ly alternating whispering and shouting, as he announces that not even God can
take Leonora from him

CONTE
Per me ora fatale,
i tuoi momenti
affretta, affretta:
la gioia che m'aspetta,
gioia mortal, no, no, no, non è!
Invano un Dio rivale
s'oppone all'amor mio,
non può nemmeno un Dio,
donna, rapirti a me,
non può rapirti a me!

COUNT
Hour, fatal for me,
speed, speed
on your moments;
the joy that awaits me is not mortal joy,
is not mortal joy, no!
In vain a rival God
opposes my love,
not even a God is able,
O woman, to steal you from me,
is able to steal you from me!

FERRANDO e SEGUACI
Ardir! andiam, ecc.

FERRANDO AND RETAINERS
Courage! let's go, etc.

CONTE
Per me ora fatale, ecc.

COUNT
Hour, fatal for me, etc.

FERRANDO e SEGUACI
Ardir! andiam, ecc.

FERRANDO AND RETAINERS
Courage! let's go, etc.

CONTE
Non può nemmen un Dio,
donna, rapirti a me, ecc.

COUNT
Not even a God is able,
O woman, to steal you from me, etc.

(The Count hides with the others. Voices of nuns are heard from within)

MONACHE
Ah! se l'error t'ingombra,
o figlia d'Eva, i rai,
presso a morir, vedrai
che un'ombra, un sogno fu:
anzi del sogno un'ombra
la speme di quaggiù!

CONTE
No, no, non può nemmeno un Dio, ecc.

FERRANDO E SEGUACI
Coraggio, ardir! ecc.

MONACHE
Vieni, e t'asconda il velo
ad ogni sguardo umano;
aura o pensier mondano
qui vivo più non è!
Al ciel ti volgi, e il cielo
si schiuderà per te.

CONTE
No, no, non può nemmen un Dio, ecc.

FERRANDO E SEGUACI
Coraggio! ardir, ecc.

MONACHE
Al ciel ti volgi, e il cielo
si schiuderà per te, ecc.

NUNS
Ah! daughter of Eve,
if error blinds your eyes,
as death nears you'll see
that it was a shadow, a dream:
nay, but the shadow of a dream
is our yearning here below!

COUNT
No, no, not even a God is able, etc.

FERRANDO AND RETAINERS
Courage! etc.

NUNS
Come, let the veil hide you
from every human eye,
no worldly air or thought
can live in here any more!
Turn to heaven, and heaven
will be disclosed to you.

COUNT
No, no, not even a God is able, etc.

FERRANDO AND RETAINERS
Courage, etc.

NUNS
Turn to heaven, and heaven
will be disclosed to you, etc.

(Leonora and Ines enter with a train of women.)

LEONORA
Perché piangete?

INES
Ah! dunque tu per sempre ne lasci!

LEONORA
O dolci amiche,
un riso, una speranza, un fior
la terra non ha per me!
Degg'io volgermi
a Quei che degli afflitti
è solo sostegno,
e dopo i penitenti giorni,
può fra gli eletti
al mio perduto bene
ricongiungermi un dì!
Tergete i rai,
e guidatemi all'ara!

CONTE *(irrompendo)*
No! giammai!

INES E **DONNE**
Il Conte!

LEONORA
Giusto ciel!

CONTE
Per te non havvi che l'ara d'imeneo.

INES E **DONNE**
Cotanto ardia!

LEONORA
Why are you weeping?

INES
Ah, then you are leaving us forever!

LEONORA
O sweet friends, earth
no longer has for me
laughter, hope or flowers!
I must turn now to Him,
who is the only
support of the grieving,
who, after my days of penance,
can join me
to my lost love
one day, among the blessed!
Dry your eyes,
and lead me to the altar!

COUNT *(bursting in)*
No, never!

INES AND **WOMEN**
The Count!

LEONORA
Merciful heaven!

COUNT
The only altar for you is the nuptial altar.

INES AND **WOMEN**
He dared go so far!

LEONORA
Insano! E qui venisti?

LEONORA
Madman! You've come here?

CONTE
A farti mia!

COUNT
To make you minc!

(The Troubadour appears.)

TUTTI
Ah!

ALL
Ah!

disc no. 1/track 29

LEONORA
E deggio e posso crederlo?
Ti veggo a me d'accanto!
È questo un sogno, un'estasi,
un sovrumano incanto!
Non regge a tanto giubilo
rapito il cor, sorpreso!
Sei tu dal ciel disceso,
o in ciel son io con te?
Sei tu dal ciel disceso, ecc.

LEONORA
Must I, can I believe it?
I see you at my side!
This is a dream, an ecstasy,
a supernatural enchantment!
My heart surprised, transported,
cannot bear such joy!
Have you come down from heaven,
or am I in heaven with you?
Have you come down from heaven, etc.

CONTE
Dunque gli estinti lasciano
di morte il regno eterno!

COUNT
So the dead can leave
death's eternal realm!

MANRICO
Né m'ebbe il ciel né l'orrido
varco infernal sentiero.

MANRICO
Heaven did not hold me, nor did
the horrid path of hell.

CONTE
A danno mio rinunzia
le prede sue l'inferno!

COUNT
Hell gives up its prey
in order to do me harm.

MANRICO
Infami sgherri vibrano
mortali colpi, è vero!

MANRICO
Your foul killers struck
mortal blows, it's true!

CONTE
Ma se non mai si fransero,
de' giorni tuoi gli stami,
se vivi e viver brami,
fuggi da lei, da me.

MANRICO
Potenza irresistibile
hanno de' fiumi l'onde!
Ma gli empî un Dio confonde!
Quel Dio soccorse a me!

LEONORA
O in ciel son io con te?
È questo un sogno, un sogno, un'estasi!
Sei tu dal ciel disceso,
o in ciel son io con te? ecc.

INES E MONACHE
Il ciel in cui fidasti
pietade avea di te, ecc.

MANRICO
Ma gli empî un Dio confonde!
Quel Dio soccorse a me! ecc.

CONTE
Se vivi e viver brami,
fuggi da lei, da me, ecc.

FERRANDO E SEGUACI DEL CONTE
(al Conte)
Tu col destin contrasti:
suo difensore egli è, ecc.

COUNT
But if it never broke,
the thread of your days,
if you live and want to live,
flee from her, and from me.

MANRICO
The waves of the rivers
have an irresistible force!
But a God confounds the wicked!
And the God succoured me!

LEONORA
Or am I in heaven with you?
This is a dream, an ecstasy!
Have you come down from heaven
or am I in heaven with you? etc.

INES AND NUNS
The heaven that you trusted
had mercy on you, etc.

MANRICO
But a God confounds the wicked!
And that God succoured me! etc.

COUNT
If you live and want to live,
flee from her, and from me, etc.

FERRANDO AND THE COUNT'S MEN
(to the Count)
You're fighting against fate,
which is defending her, etc.

(Ruiz enters with armed men)

RUIZ E SEGUACI DI MANRICO
Urgel viva!

MANRICO
Miei prodi guerrieri!

RUIZ
Vieni!

MANRICO
Donna, mi segui.

CONTE
E tu speri?

LEONORA
Ah!

MANRICO
T'arretra!

CONTE
Involarmi costei? No!

RUIZ AND MANRICO'S RETAINERS
Long live Urgel!

MANRICO
My brave fighters!

RUIZ
Come!

MANRICO
My lady, follow me.

COUNT
You dare hope?

LEONORA
Ah!

MANRICO
Stand back!

COUNT
To steal her from me? No!

(The Count draws his sword, but is disarmed by Ruiz and his men.)

RUIZ E UOMINI
Vaneggia!

FERRANDO E SEGUACI
Che tenti, signor?

CONTE
Di ragione ogni lume perdei!
Ho le furie nel cor! ecc.

RUIZ AND MEN
He's raving!

FERRANDO AND RETAINERS
What are you attempting, Sir?

COUNT
I lost my reason!
My heart is raging! etc.

LEONORA
M'atterrisce! ecc.

INES E DONNE
Ah, sì, il ciel pietade avea di te! –

MANRICO
Fia supplizio la vita per te! ecc.

RUIZ E SEGUACI DI MANRICO
Vieni, la sorte sorride per te, ecc.

FERRANDO E SEGUACI DEL CONTE
Cedi; or ceder
viltade non è! ecc.

LEONORA
Sei tu dal ciel disceso,
o in ciel son io con te?
Con te, in ciel con te?

INES E DONNE
Pietade avea di te!

MANRICO E SEGUACI
Vieni, ah vieni, vieni, vieni!

CONTE
Ho le furie in cor!

SEGUACI DEL CONTE
Cedi! ah cedi, cedi!

LEONORA
He terrifies me!

INES AND WOMEN
Ah yes, heaven had mercy on you! –

MANRICO
May your life be a torment! etc.

RUIZ AND MANRICO'S RETAINERS
Come; Fate smiles on you, etc.

FERRANDO & THE COUNT'S RETAINERS
Surrender; to surrender now
is not cowardice! etc.

LEONORA
Have you come down from heaven,
or am I in heaven with you?
With you, in heaven with you?

INES AND WOMEN
—had mercy upon you!

MANRICO AND RETAINERS
Come! ah, come, come, come!

COUNT
My heart is raging!

THE COUNT'S RETAINERS
Surrender, ah, surrender, surrender!

(Manrico goes off with Leonora. The women take refuge in the convent)

Act Three

SCENE ONE

disc no. 2/track 1 A military camp. On the right, the Count di Luna's tent, over which flies the commander's pennon. Squads of soldiers are everywhere. Others are gambling; still other are strolling. Then Ferrando comes out of the Count's tent.

ALCUNI SOLDATI
Or co' dadi, ma fra poco
giuocherem ben altro giuoco.
Quest'acciar, dal sangue or terso,
fia di sangue in breve asperso!

(other soldiers arrive)

Il soccorso dimandato!
Han l'aspetto del valor!
Più l'assalto ritardato
or non fia di Castellor.
Più l'assalto, ecc.

FERRANDO
Sì, prodi amici; al dì novello
è mente del capitan la rocca
investir da ogni parte.
Colà pingue bottino
certezza è rinvenir, più che speranza.
Si vinca; è nostro.

SOME SOLDIERS
Now we're dicing, but ere long
we'll play a quite different game;
this sword, now wiped clean of blood,
will soon be bathed in blood again!

The reinforcements asked for!
They look brave enough!
May the attack on Castellor
no longer be put off.
May the attack, etc.

FERRANDO
Yes, brave friends, at dawn
the captain plans to attack
the fort on every side.
There rich booty
we'll surely find, beyond our hopes.
Conquer then, and it's ours.

SOLDATI
Tu c'inviti a danza!

TUTTI
Squilli, echeggi la tromba guerriera,
chiami all'armi, alla pugna, all'assalto;
fia domani la nostra bandiera
di quei merli piantata sull'alto.
No, giammai non sorrise vittoria
di più liete speranze finor!
Ivi l'util ci aspetta e la gloria,
ivi opimi la preda e l'onor.
Squilli, echeggi, ecc.
No, giammai non sorrise vittoria, ecc.

SOLDIERS
You're inviting us to a party.

ALL
Let the warlike trumpet sound and echo,
call to arms, to the fray, the attack;
may our flag be planted tomorrow
on the highest of those towers.
No, victory has never smiled
on happier hopes than ours!
There glory awaits us – and the needful.
There wait spoil, booty and honour.
Let the warlike trumpet, etc.
No, victory has never smiled etc.

(They disperse. The Count comes out of his tent)

disc no. 2/track 2

CONTE
In braccio al mio rival!
Questo pensiero come persecutor demone
ovunque m'insegue.
In braccio al mio rival!
Ma corro, surta appena l'aurora,
io corro a separarvi.
Oh Leonora!

COUNT
In my rival's arms!
This thought pursues me everywhere
like a persecuting demon.
In my rival's arms!
But as soon as dawn breaks, I'll run,
I'll run to separate you.
Oh Leonora!

(Ferrando enters)

Che fu?

What is it?

FERRANDO
D'appresso al campo
s'aggirava una zingara;
sorpresa da' nostri esploratori,
si volse in fuga; essi a ragion

FERRANDO
Near the camp
a gypsy was wandering:
surprised by our scouts,
she started to flee; rightfully

temendo una spia nella trista,
l'inseguîr.

CONTE
Fu raggiunta?

FERRANDO
È presa.

CONTE
Vista l'hai tu?

FERRANDO
No. Della scorta il condottier
m'apprese l'evento.

(noises are heard)

CONTE
Eccola.

(Azucena is dragged before the Count)

SOLDATI
Innanzi, o strega, innanzi!
Innanzi! innanzi!

AZUCENA
Aita! mi lasciate! Ah furibondi!
Che mal fec'io?

CONTE
S'appressi.
A me rispondi,
e trema dal mentir!

AZUCENA
Chiedi.

fearing the wretch was a spy,
they followed her.

COUNT
Did they overtake her?

FERRANDO
She's been taken.

COUNT
Have you seen her?

FERRANDO
No. The commander of the patrol
gave me the news.

COUNT
Here she is.

SOLDIERS
Forward, you witch, forward!
Forward! Forward!

AZUCENA
Help! let me go! Ah, you raving men!
What have I done wrong?

COUNT
Approach.
Answer me,
and don't dare lie to me!

AZUCENA
Question me.

CONTE
Ove vai?

AZUCENA
Nol so.

CONTE
Che?

AZUCENA
D'una zingara è costume
mover senza disegno
il passo vagabondo,
ed è suo tetto il ciel,
sua patria il mondo.

CONTE
E vieni?

AZUCENA
Da Biscaglia, ove finora
le sterili montagne ebbi a ricetto.

CONTE
(Da Biscaglia!)

FERRANDO
(Che intesi! Oh qual sospetto!)

disc no. 2/track 3

AZUCENA
Giorni poveri vivea,
pur contenta del mio stato,
sola speme un figlio avea.
Mi lasciò, m'oblia, l'ingrato!
Io, deserta, vado errando
di quel figlio ricercando,

COUNT
Where are you going?

AZUCENA
I don't know.

COUNT
What?

AZUCENA
It's the gypsy's custom
to move her wandering steps
without any plan;
the sky is her roof,
and the world is her country.

COUNT
Where have you come from?

AZUCENA
From Biscay, whose barren mountains
received me until now.

COUNT
(From Biscay!)

FERRANDO
(What do I hear! Oh, what a suspicion!)

AZUCENA
I lived days of poverty,
yet happy in my condition,
my only hope was my son.
The ingrate left and forgot me!
Abandoned, I wander about,
hunting for that son,

di quel figlio che al mio core
pene orribili costò!
Qual per esso provo amore
madre in terra non provò!

FERRANDO
(Il suo volto!)

CONTE
Di', traesti lunga etade
fra quei monti?

AZUCENA
Lunga sì.

CONTE
Rammenteresti un fanciul, prole di conti,
involato al suo castello,
son tre lustri, e tratto quivi?

AZUCENA
E tu...parla...sei?

CONTE
Fratello del rapito!

AZUCENA
(Ah!)

FERRANDO
(Sì!)

CONTE
Ne udivi mai novella?

AZUCENA
Io! no! concedi
che del figlio l'orme io scopra.

for that son who cost my heart
horrible pangs!
The love I feel for him
no other mother on earth has felt!

FERRANDO
(Her face!)

COUNT
Tell me: did you stay a long time
in those mountains?

AZUCENA
Yes, a long time.

COUNT
Can you remember a child,
a Count's son, stolen from his castle
fifteen years ago, and brought thither?

AZUCENA
You...speak...who are you?

COUNT
The stolen boy's brother!

AZUCENA
(Ah!)

FERRANDO
(Yes!)

COUNT
Did you ever hear the story?

AZUCENA
Not I! Let me
follow my son's footsteps.

FERRANDO
Resta, iniqua!

AZUCENA
(Ohimè!)

FERRANDO *(al Conte)*
Tu vedi chi l'infame,
orribil opra commettea.

CONTE
Finisci.

FERRANDO
È dessa!

AZUCENA
Taci!

FERRANDO
È dessa che il bambino arse!

CONTE
Ah, perfida!

SOLDATI
Ella stessa!

AZUCENA
Ei mentisce!

CONTE
Al tuo destino or non fuggi!

AZUCENA
Deh!

FERRANDO
Wait, foul wretch!

AZUCENA
(Alas!)

FERRANDO *(to the Count)*
You see who committed
the horrible, ghastly deed.

COUNT
Go on.

FERRANDO
She's the one!

AZUCENA
Be silent!

FERRANDO
She's the one who burned the child!

COUNT
Ah, monster!

SOLDIERS
She's the one!

AZUCENA
He's lying!

COUNT
Now you won't escape your fate!

AZUCENA
I beg you!

CONTE
Quei nodi più stringete!

AZUCENA
Oh Dio! oh Dio!

SOLDATI
Urla pur!

AZUCENA
E tu non vieni, o Manrico,
O figlio mio?
Non soccorri
all'infelice madre tua?

CONTE
Di Manrico genitrice!

FERRANDO
Trema!

CONTE
Oh sorte! In mio poter!

FERRANDO
Trema! Trema!

CONTE
Oh, sorte!

AZUCENA
Deh! rallentate, o barbari,
le acerbe mie ritorte.
Questo crudel supplizio
è prolungata morte!
D'iniquo genitore
empio figliuol peggiore,

COUNT
Tie those knots tighter!

AZUCENA
Oh God! Oh God!

SOLDIERS
Go ahead and shout!

AZUCENA
Why don't you come, Manrico,
O my son?
Won't you aid
your wretched mother?

COUNT
Manrico's mother!

FERRANDO
Quake!

COUNT
Oh luck! She's in my power!

FERRANDO
Quake! Quake!

COUNT
Oh, luck!

AZUCENA
Ah! Pray, loosen, barbarians,
the chains that bite me so.
This cruel torture
is like a drawn-out death!
Oh wicked son, worse
than your wicked father,

trema! V'è Dio pei miseri,
v'è Dio pei miseri,
trema! V'è Dio,
e Dio ti punirà, ah, sì, ah, sì, ecc.

beware! God protects the helpless,
and God will punish you!

disc no. 2/track 4 Azucena, in chains and about to be burnt at the stake like her mother, is one huge bundle of rage here. In just under two minutes she manages to express her hatred twice, while the Count, singing just as quickly and maniacally, is as vicious as she is. The horns underline every breathless word uttered, and the scene ends in a frenzy.

CONTE

Tua prole, o turpe zingara,
colui, quel seduttore?
Potrò col tuo supplizio
ferirlo in mezzo al cor!
Gioia m'inonda il petto,
cui non esprime il detto!
Ah, meco il fraterno cenere
piena vendetta avrà!

COUNT

Your brood, foul gypsy,
he? That seducer?
With your torture then
I can wound his heart!
Joy floods my breast,
which words cannot express!
Ah, through me, my brother's ashes
will have complete vengeance!

FERRANDO e SOLDATI

Infame, pira sorgere,
ah sì! vedrai tra poco.
Né solo tuo supplizio
sarà terreno foco!
Le vampe dell'inferno
a te fian rogo eterno!
Ivi penare ed ardere
l'alma dovrà!

FERRANDO and SOLDIERS

Wretch, you'll see a pyre
rise here in a little while.
Nor will the earthly fire
be your only punishment!
The flames of hell for you
will be an eternal stake!
There your soul will have
to suffer and to burn!

AZUCENA

Deh! rallentate, o barbari,
le acerbe mie ritorte.
Questo crudel supplizio
è prolungata morte!
D'iniquo genitore

AZUCENA

Pray loosen, barbarians,
the chains that bite me so.
This cruel torture
is like a drawn-out death!
O wicked son, worse

empio figliuol peggiore,
trema! V'è Dio pei miseri,
v'è Dio pei miseri,
trema! V'è Dio,
e Dio ti punirà, ah, sì, ah, sì, ecc.

than your wicked father,
beware! God protects the helpless,
God protects the helpless,
beware! There is a God,
and God will punish you, ah yes, ah yes, etc.

CONTE

Tua prole, o turpe zingara,
colui, quel seduttore?
Meco il fraterno cenere
piena vendetta avrà, ecc.

COUNT

Your brood, foul gypsy,
he? That seducer?
Through me, my brother's ashes
will have complete vengeance! etc.

FERRANDO E SOLDATI

Le vampe dell'inferno
a te fia rogo eterno!
Ivi penare ed ardere
l'alma dovrà! ecc.

FERRANDO AND SOLDIERS

The flames of hell for you
will be an eternal stake!
There your soul will have
to suffer and to burn! etc.

(at a sign from the Count, the soldiers drag Azucena away)

SCENE TWO

disc no. 2/track 5

LEONORA

Quale d'armi fragor poc'anzi intesi?

LEONORA

What was that sound of arms I heard a
moment ago?

MANRICO

Alto è il periglio:
vano dissimularlo fora!
Alla novella aurora
assaliti saremo.

MANRICO

The danger is great:
no use to disguise it!
At dawn tomorrow
we'll be attacked.

LEONORA

Ahimè! Che dici?

LEONORA

Alas! What are you saying?

MANRICO
Ma de' nostri nemici
avrem vittoria. Pari
abbiamo al loro ardir,
brando, e coraggio.
(a Ruiz)
Tu va. Le belliche opre,
nell'assenza mia breve,
a te commetto.
Che nulla manchi.

(Ruiz leaves)

LEONORA
Di qual tetra luce
il nostro imen risplende!

MANRICO
Il presagio funesto,
deh, sperdi, o cara!

LEONORA
E il posso?

MANRICO
Amor, sublime amore,
in tale istante ti favelli al core.

MANRICO
But we will vanquish
our enemies. Our daring,
our arms, and our courage
are equal to theirs.
(to Ruiz)
Go. During my short absence,
I commit to your care
the warlike work.
Let nothing be missing.

LEONORA
What a grim light
shines on our wedding!

MANRICO
Ah, my dear, rid yourself
of any gloomy forebodings!

LEONORA
How can I?

MANRICO
Let love, sublime love, at this moment
speak to your heart.

disc 2/track 6   Manrico is at his most elegant and eloquent in this exquisite, almost old-fash-
ioned aria to his love of Leonora. It requires singing of great sensitivity, fine
breath control and even a trill at the word "parra." Only once more in the opera
will we hear Manrico express himself with such loveliness, and that will be in the
final scene, with his mother (track 19).

Ah sì, ben mio, coll'essere
io tuo, tu mia consorte,
avrò più l'alma intrepida,
il braccio avrò più forte.

Ah yes, my love, when I'll be
yours, and you'll be mine,
my spirit will be more fearless,
my arm will be stronger.

97

Ma pur, se nella pagina
de' miei destini è scritto
ch'io resti fra le vittime,
dal ferro ostil trafitto,
fra quegli estremi aneliti
a te il pensier verrà,
e solo in ciel precederti
la morte a me parrà.
E solo in ciel precederti, ecc.
(Si sente l'organo dalla cappella)

And yet, if on the page
of my destiny it's written
that I must be among the victims,
pierced by the foe's steel,
as I draw my last breath,
my thoughts will come to you,
and death will seem to me
only preceding you to heaven.
And death will seem to me, etc.
(The chapel organ is heard)

disc no. 2/track 7

LEONORA E MANRICO
L'onda de' suoni mistici
pura discenda al cor!
Vieni, ci schiude il tempio
gioie di casto amor!
Ah! Gioie di casto amor! ecc.

LEONORA AND MANRICO
The wave of holy sounds
descends, pure, into our hearts!
Come, the altar opens to us
the joys of unspoiled love!
Ah! the joys of unspoiled love etc.

(Ruiz runs in)

RUIZ
Manrico?

RUIZ
Manrico?

MANRICO
Che?

MANRICO
What is it?

RUIZ
La zingara...vieni...tra' ceppi mira...

RUIZ
The gypsy...come...in irons...look...

MANRICO
Oh Dio!

MANRICO
Oh God!

RUIZ
Per man de' barbari
accesa è già la pira...

RUIZ
Those barbarians' hands
have already lighted the pyre...

MANRICO *(accostandosi al verone)*
Oh ciel! Mie membra oscillano.
Nube mi copre il ciglio!

LEONORA
Tu fremi!

MANRICO
E il deggio!
Sappilo: io son –

LEONORA
Chi mai?

MANRICO
Suo figlio!

LEONORA
Ah!

MANRICO
Ah, vili! Il rio spettacolo
quasi il respir m'invola!
Raduna i nostri! Affrettati,
Ruiz! Va, va...Torna, vola!

MANRICO *(approaching the balcony)*
Heaven! My legs fail me,
my eyes are clouding over!

LEONORA
You're raging!

MANRICO
I should!
Learn then: I am –

LEONORA
Who?

MANRICO
Her son!

LEONORA
Ah!

MANRICO
Ah, cowards! This wicked sight
almost takes away my breath!
Get our men together! Hurry
Ruiz! Go, go...And fly back!

(Ruiz leaves)

disc no. 2/track 8 Having finished what must be the shortest love duet in opera (track 7), Manrico,
roused from his happiness by news of his mother's imminent conflagration,
launches into one of the most eagerly awaited displays in all of Italian opera. Here
he proves himself to be a tenor of heroic proportions. The choppy, short phrases
up against the orchestra's insistent forte are all anxiety and resolve, and while
Verdi did not write the high Cs you will hear here (and will rarely hear performed as
well), he did not disapprove. "Far be it from me to deny the public what it wants,"
he said—and the public wants the act to end in a display of glorious sound.

Di quella pira, l'orrendo foco
tutte le fibre m'arse, avvampò!
Empî, spegnetela, o ch'io fra poco
col sangue vostro la spegnerò!
Era già figlio prima d'amarti,
non può frenarmi il tuo martir...
Madre infelice, corro a salvarti,
o teco almeno corro a morir!

LEONORA
Non reggo a colpi tanto funesti.
Oh, quanto meglio saria morir!

MANRICO
Di quella pira, ecc.

(Ruiz comes back with the soldiers)

RUIZ e SOLDATI
All'armi! All'armi!
Eccone presti a pugnar teco,
o teco a morir!
All'armi! ecc.

MANRICO
Madre infelice, corro a salvarti,
o teco almeno corro a morir! ecc.
All'armi! All'armi! All'armi!

(They leave)

The horrible blaze of that pyre
burns, enflames all of my being!
Monsters, put it out; or very quickly
I'll put it out with your blood!
Before I loved you, I was yet her son;
your suffering cannot restrain me...
Unhappy mother, I hasten to save you,
or at least, hasten to die with you!

LEONORA
I cannot bear such deadly blows.
Oh, how much better to die!

MANRICO
The horrible blaze of that pyre, etc.

RUIZ and SOLDIERS
To arms! To arms!
Here we are, ready to fight with you,
or die with you!
To arms, etc.

MANRICO
Unhappy mother, I hasten to save you,
Or at least hasten to die with you! etc.
To arms! To arms! To arms!

Act 4

SCENE ONE

disc no. 2/track 9 A wing of the Aliaferia palace; at one corner a tower with windows. Very dark night. Two people come in, muffled in cloaks: Ruiz and Leonora.

RUIZ
Siam giunti; ecco la torre,
ove di Stato gemono i prigionieri.
Ah! l'infelice ivi fu tratto!

RUIZ
We've arrived; there's the tower,
where the State's prisoners languish.
Ah, the hapless man was brought here!

LEONORA
Vanne...lasciami,
né timor di me ti prenda.
Salvarlo io potrò, forse.

LEONORA
Go...leave me,
and don't fear for me.
I can save him, perhaps.

(Ruiz retires.)

Timor di me?...Sicura,
presta è la mia difesa.

Fear for me?...Sure
and ready is my protection.

(She looks at a ring on her right hand.)

In quest'oscura notte ravvolta,
presso a te son io, e tu nol sai!
Gemente aura, che intorno spiri,
deh, pietosa gli arreca i miei sospiri.

Shrouded in this dark night,
I'm near you, and you don't know it!
Moaning wind, you who blow here,
ah, mercifully take my sights to him.

disc no. 2/track 10 It is in this aria that one might define the so-called "Verdi soprano." Long, arched melody, a vocal line which stretches higher and higher in exposed (i.e: lightly accompanied by the orchestra) phrases—some of them marked to be sung very softly—and an innate sadness tell us all about Leonora's state of mind at this point.

D'amor sull'ali rosee	On the rosy wings of love
vanne, sospir dolente;	go, oh mournful sigh;
del prigioniero misero	comfort the flagging spirits
conforta l'egra mente.	of the wretched prisoner.
Com'aura di speranza	Like a breath of hope
aleggia in quella stanza;	flutter in that room;
lo desta alle memorie,	waken in him the memories,
ai sogni, ai sogni dell'amor.	the dreams, the dreams of love.
Ma, deh! non dirgli improvvido	But, pray, don't imprudently tell him
le pene, le pene del mio cor! ecc.	the pangs, the pangs that rack my heart! etc.

disc no. 2/track 11 Monks intone gloomily, Manrico sings from off-stage with tragic defiance, pleading with Leonora not to forget him, as Leonora, practically broken, sings in descending, mournful phrases.

FRATI (*dall'interno*)
Miserere d'un'alma già vicina
alla partenza che non ha ritorno.
Miserere di lei, bontà divina,
preda non sia dell'infernal soggiorno.

MONKS (*from within*)
Have mercy on a spirit approaching
the departure which has no return.
Have mercy on him, divine Goodness.
Keep him from being the prey of hell.

LEONORA
Quel suon, quelle preci
solenni, funeste,
empiron quest'aere
di cupo terror!
Contende l'ambascia,
che tutta m'investe,
al labbro il respiro,
i palpiti al cor!

LEONORA
That sound, those prayers,
so solemn and dire,
fill the air
with baleful terror!
The distress
that fills me almost deprives
my lips of their breath,
my heart of its beating!

MANRICO (*dalla torre*)
Ah! che la morte ognora
è tarda nel venir,

MANRICO (*from the tower*)
Ah! how slow Death
is in its coming,

a chi desìa morir!
Addio, addio Leonora, addio!

LEONORA
Oh ciel! Sento mancarmi!

FRATI
Miserere, ecc.

LEONORA
Sull'orrida torre,
ahi, par che la morte
con ali di tenebre
librando si va!
Ahi! forse dischiuse
gli fian queste porte
sol quando cadaver
già freddo sarà!

FRATI
Miserere...miserere...miserere...

MANRICO
Sconto col sangue mio
l'amor che posi in te!
Non ti scordar, non ti scordar di me,
Leonora, addio! Leonora, addio!

LEONORA
Di, te, di te scordarmi!
Sento mancarmi! ecc.

MANRICO
Sconto col sangue mio, ecc.

FRATI
Miserere...miserere...miserere...

to him who longs to die!
Farewell, Leonora, Farewell!

LEONORA
Oh heaven! I feel faint!

MONKS
Have mercy, etc.

LEONORA
Over the horrid tower,
ah, Death seems
with wings of darkness
to be poised!
Ah, perhaps these doors
will be opened for him,
only when his corpse
is already cold!

MONKS
Have mercy...have mercy...have mercy...

MANRICO
I'm paying with my blood
for the love I bore you!
Don't forget, don't forget me,
Leonora, farewell, Leonora, farewell!

LEONORA
Forget you! Forget you!
I feel faint! etc.

MANRICO
I'm paying with my blood, etc.

MONKS
Have mercy...have mercy...have mercy...

LEONORA
Di te, di te scordarmi!
Tu vedrai che amore in terra
mai del mio non fu più forte:
vinse il fato in aspra guerra,
vincerà la stessa morte.
O col prezzo mi mia vita
la tua vita salverò,
o con te per sempre unita
nella tomba scenderò!
Tu vedrai che amore in terra, ecc.

LEONORA
How could I ever forget you!
You will see that never on earth
was there a stronger love than mine;
it defeated Fate in violent strife,
it will defeat death itself.
Either at the cost of my life
I shall save your life,
or, forever united to you
I shall descend into the grave!
You will see that never on earth, etc.

(Leonora retires. The Count comes out of the palace with some guards.)

CONTE
Udiste?
Come albeggi, la scure al figlio,
ed alla madre il rogo.

COUNT
Did you hear?
As dawn breaks, the son to the block,
and the mother to the stake.

(The guards go into the tower.)

Abuso forse quel poter
che pieno in me trasmise il prence!
A tal mi traggi,
donna per me funesta!
Ov'ella è mai?
Ripreso Castellor,
di lei contezza non ebbi,
e furo indarno tante ricerche e tante!
Ah, dove sei, crudele?

Perhaps I'm abusing the power
that the Prince freely gave me!
That's what you drive me to,
O my fatal woman!
Where can she be?
When Castellor was retaken,
I had no word of her,
and all our searching was in vain!
Ah, where are you, cruel one?

(Leonora reveals herself.)

LEONORA
A te davante.

LEONORA
Before you.

CONTE
Qual voce! Come? Tu, donna?

LEONORA
Il vedi.

CONTE
A che venisti?

LEONORA
Egli è già presso all'ora estrema,
e tu lo chiedi?

CONTE
Osar potresti?

LEONORA
Ah sì, per esso pietà domando!

CONTE
Che? Tu deliri!

LEONORA
Pietà!

CONTE
Tu deliri!

LEONORA
Pietà!

CONTE
Ah! io del rival sentir pietà?

LEONORA
Clemente Nume a te l'ispiri!

COUNT
That voice! What? You, woman?

LEONORA
As you see.

COUNT
Why have you come?

LEONORA
His last hour is approaching,
and you ask me?

COUNT
You dared?

LEONORA
Ah yes, I ask mercy for him!

COUNT
What? You're raving!

LEONORA
Mercy!

COUNT
You're raving!

LEONORA
Mercy!

COUNT
I? Show mercy to my rival?

LEONORA
A clement God inspire you!

CONTE
Ah! io del rival sentir pietà?

LEONORA
Clemente Nume a te l'ispiri!

CONTE
È sol vendetta il mio Nume, ecc.

LEONORA
Pietà! Pietà! Domando pietà!

CONTE
Va!...va!...va!...

COUNT
I? Show mercy to my rival?

LEONORA
A clement God inspire you!

COUNT
Vengeance is my only god, etc.

LEONORA
Pity! Pity! I ask pity!

COUNT
Go!...Go!...Go!...

**disc no. 2/
track 14-16**

This is only duet Leonora sings with the Count, and in it, her love for Manrico allows her to regather her strength. The orchestra moves along with the rhythm of a steam locomotive while she goes through every grotesque offer she can to win Manrico's freedom; di Luna, just as insistently, sadistically refuses. In track 15, Leonora pulls the last of her punches—she offers herself to di Luna in return for Manrico's life, but at **01:01** she takes poison and let's us in on her secret—all di Luna will have of her is a lifeless corpse. By track 16, Leonora practically sounds giddy—a not incongruous concept for a woman who values her lover's life more than her own—and the scene ends in triumph, albeit a bloody triumph.

LEONORA
Mira, d'acerbe lagrime
spargo al tuo piede un rio;
non basta il pianto?
Svenami, ti bevi il sangue mio.
Calpesta il mio cadavere,
ma salva il Trovator!

CONTE
Ah! dell'indegno rendere
vorrei peggior la sorte,

LEONORA
Look, at your feet I shed
a river of bitter tears;
Isn't my weeping enough?
Then stab me and drink my blood,
trample upon my corpse,
but save the Troubadour!

COUNT
Ah! I would like to make worse
the unworthy man's fate,

fra mille atroci spasimi
centuplicar sua morte.

LEONORA
Svenami...

CONTE
Più l'ami e più terribile
divampa il mio furor!

LEONORA
Calpesta il mio cadavere,
ma salva il Trovator!

CONTE
Più l'ami e più terribile
divampa il mio furor! ecc.

LEONORA
Mi svena, mi svena, calpesta il mio cadaver,
ma salva il Trovator, ecc.

disc no. 2/track 15

LEONORA
Conte!

CONTE
Né basti!

LEONORA
Grazia!

CONTE
Prezzo non avvi alcuno ad ottenerla.
Scostati!

make him die a hundred deaths
in a hundred horrible spasms.

LEONORA
Then stab me...

COUNT
The more you love him, the worse
my fury flames up!

LEONORA
Triumph upon my corpse,
but save the Troubadour!

COUNT
The more you love him, the worse
my fury flames up! etc.

LEONORA
Stab me, stab me, triumph upon my corpse,
but save the Troubadour! etc.

LEONORA
Count!

COUNT
Won't you stop?

LEONORA
Spare him!

COUNT
At no price could you gain that.
Move away!

LEONORA
Uno ve n'ha, sol uno,
ed io te l'offro!

CONTE
Spiegati, qual prezzo, di'?

LEONORA
Me stessa!

CONTE
Ciel! Tu dicesti?

LEONORA
E compiere saprò la mia promessa.

CONTE
È sogno il mio?

LEONORA
Dischiudimi la via fra quelle mura;
ch'ei m'oda, che la vittima fugga,
e son tua.

CONTE
Lo giura.

LEONORA
Lo giuro a Dio,
che l'anima tutta mi vede.

CONTE
Olà!

LEONORA
There is one price, just one;
and I'll give it to you!

COUNT
Explain yourself. Tell me: what is this
price?

LEONORA
Myself!

COUNT
Heaven! What did you say?

LEONORA
And I will keep my promise.

COUNT
Am I dreaming?

LEONORA
Make way for me within those walls;
let him hear me, let the victim flee,
and I am yours.

COUNT
Swear it.

LEONORA
I swear before God,
who can see my whole soul.

COUNT
Ho there!

(A guard appears. While the Count is whispering to him, Leonora sucks the poison concealed in her ring.)

LEONORA
(M'avrai...ma fredda, esanime spoglia.)

disc no. 2/track 16

CONTE
Colui vivrà.

LEONORA
(Vivrà! Contende il giubilo
i detti a me, Signore,
ma coi frequenti palpiti
mercè ti rende il core!
Or il mio fine impavida,
piena di gioia attendo,
potrò dirgli morendo,
salvo tu sei per me!)

CONTE
Fra te che parli? Volgimi,
mi volgi il detto ancora,
o mi parrà delirio
quanto ascoltai finora!

LEONORA
Vivrà!

CONTE
Tu mia! tu mia! ripetilo,
il dubbio cor serena,
ah! ch'io credo appena
udendolo da te!

LEONORA
Vivrà! Contende il giubilo
i detti a me, Signore,
potrò dirgli morendo:

LEONORA
(You'll have me...but as a cold and lifeless
corpse.)

COUNT
He shall live.

LEONORA
(He'll live! My joy strips me
of words. O Lord,
but with its hurried beating
my heart renders thanks!
Now, fearless, filled with joy
I can await the end,
dying I can tell him:
I have saved you!)

COUNT
What are you whispering? Turn,
turn your words to me again,
or it will all seem a dream –
what I heard before!

LEONORA
He'll live!

COUNT
You're mine! Mine! Repeat it,
reassure my doubting heart;
ah, I can scarcely believe it,
when I hear it from you!

LEONORA
He'll live! My joy strips me
of words, O Lord.
Dying I can tell him:

salvo tu sei per me!
Salvo tu sei, tu sei per me! Ah! ecc.

CONTE
Tu mia, tu mia, ah!
Ch'io lo credo appena! ecc.

LEONORA
Andiam!

CONTE
Giurasti –

LEONORA
Andiam!

CONTE
Pensaci!

LEONORA
È sacra la mia fè!

LEONORA
Vivrà! Contende il giubilo, ecc.

CONTE
Tu mia! tu mia! ripetilo, ecc.

I have saved you!
I have saved you! Ah! etc.

COUNT
You're mine, mine, ah!
I can scarcely believe it! etc.

LEONORA
Let us go!

COUNT
You've sworn –

LEONORA
Let us go!

COUNT
 – Remember!

LEONORA
My word is sacred!

LEONORA
He'll live! My joy strips me, etc.

COUNT
You're mine! You're mine! repeat it, etc.

(They go into the tower.)

SCENE TWO

disc no. 2/track 17 A horrible dungeon; in one corner a barred window. Azucena lies on a kind of rough coverlet. Manrico is sitting beside her.

MANRICO
Madre, non dormi?

MANRICO
Mother, can't you sleep?

AZUCENA
L'invocai, più volte,
ma fugge il sonno a queste luci!
Prego.

MANRICO
L'aura fredda è molesta
alle tue membra forse?

AZUCENA
No da questa tomba di vivi
solo fuggir vorrei,
perché sento il respiro soffocarmi.

MANRICO
Fuggir!

AZUCENA
Non attristarti:
far di me strazio
non potranno i crudi!

MANRICO
Ahi, come?

AZUCENA
Vedi? Le sue fosche impronte
m'ha già segnato in fronte
il dito della morte!

MANRICO
Ahi!

AZUCENA
Troveranno un cadavere,
muto, gelido! Anzi uno scheletro!

AZUCENA
I've invoked sleep time and again,
but it flees from my eyes!
I'm praying.

MANRICO
Perhaps the chilly air
is painful for your limbs?

AZUCENA
No, only I would like to flee from this
tomb of the living because I feel that my
breath is choking me.

MANRICO
Flee!

AZUCENA
Don't be sad;
the barbarians
won't be able to torture me!

MANRICO
What?

AZUCENA
You see, the finger of Death
has already set on my forehead
its dark prints!

MANRICO
Ah!

AZUCENA
They'll find a corpse, mute and cold!
No, a skeleton!

MANRICO
Cessa!

AZUCENA
Non odi?
Gente appressa...
I carnefici son...
Vogliono al rogo trarmi!
Difendi la tua madre!

MANRICO
Alcuno, ti rassicura.

AZUCENA
Il rogo –

MANRICO
Alcuno qui non volge.

AZUCENA
Il rogo! il rogo! il rogo!
Parola orrenda!

MANRICO
Oh madre! oh madre!

AZUCENA
Un giorno turba feroce
l'ava tua condusse al rogo!
Mira la terribil vampa!
Ella n'è tocca già!
Già l'arso crine al ciel
manda faville!
Osserva le pupille
fuor dell'orbita loro!
Ahi! chi mi toglie
a spettacolo sì atroce!

MANRICO
Stop!

AZUCENA
Don't you hear?
People are coming...
The executioners...
They want to drag me to the stake!
Defend you mother!

MANRICO
Nobody, rest assured.

AZUCENA
The stake –

MANRICO
Nobody's coming here.

AZUCENA
The stake! The stake! The stake!
That horrible word!

MANRICO
Oh Mother! Mother!

AZUCENA
One day a ferocious mob
led your grandmother to the stake!
Look at the terrible flames!
They're touching her already!
Her burning hair already
send sparks up to heaven!
Look at her eyes,
hanging out of their sockets!
Ah! who will save me
from this horrible sight!

MANRICO
Se m'ami ancor, se voce di figlio
ha possa d'una madre in seno,
ai terrori dell'alma
oblio cerca nel sonno,
e posa e calma.

MANRICO
If you love me still, if a son's voice
has power in a mother's breast,
seek oblivion in sleep
from the spirit's terrors,
and rest and calm.

AZUCENA
Sì, la stanchezza m'opprime, o figlio...
Alla quiete io chiudo il ciglio,
ma se del rogo
arder si veda l'orrida fiamma, destami allor.

AZUCENA
Yes, weariness overcomes me, my son...
I'll close my eyes in peace,
but if you see burning
the stake's horrid flames, then waken me.

MANRICO
Riposa, o madre, Iddio conceda
men tristi immagini al tuo sopor.

MANRICO
Rest now, mother, and may God
grant less grievous images to your sleep.

disc no. 2/track 19 This is the apotheosis of Manrico's loving relationship with his mother. After she once again recalls the burning, screaming, catastrophe, etc. (track 17), Manrico sings a lullaby to her and she drifts off to sleep. There is no more tender moment in all of opera: Azucena rests, thinking of returning to their mountain home in peace, as Manrico lolls her into oblivion.

AZUCENA
Ai nostri monti ritorneremo,
l'antica pace ivi godremo!
Tu canterai...sul tuo liuto,
in sonno placido io dormirò.

AZUCENA
We'll go back to our mountains,
and there enjoy our former peace!
You'll sing...with your lute,
and I'll sleep serenely.

MANRICO
Riposa, o madre, io prono
e muto la mente al cielo rivolgerò.

MANRICO
Rest, mother. Silent and alert,
I'll turn my thoughts to Heaven.

AZUCENA
Tu canterai, ecc.

AZUCENA
You'll sing, etc.

MANRICO
La mente al cielo rivolgerò, ecc.
Riposa, o madre, ecc.

MANRICO
I'll turn my thoughts to heaven,
Rest, mother, etc.

(She falls asleep. The door opens and Leonora comes in.)

disc no. 2/track 20

MANRICO
Che! Non m'inganna
quel fioco lume?

MANRICO
What! Does that feeble
light not deceive me?

LEONORA
Son io, Manrico, mio Manrico!

LEONORA
It's I, Manrico, my Manrico!

MANRICO
Oh! mia Leonora!
Ah, mi concedi, pietoso Nume,
gioia sì grande anzi ch'io mora?

MANRICO
O, my Leonora!
Ah! piteous Heaven, do you grant me
such a great joy before I die?

LEONORA
Tu non morrai; vengo a salvarti!

LEONORA
You won't die; I've come to save you!

MANRICO
Come? A salvarmi? Fia vero?

MANRICO
What? To save me? Can it be true?

LEONORA
Addio! tronca ogni indugio!
T'affretta! Parti!

LEONORA
Farewell! Don't delay!
Hurry! Leave!

MANRICO
E tu non vieni?

MANRICO
And you're not coming?

LEONORA
Restar degg'io.

LEONORA
I must stay.

MANRICO
Restar?

MANRICO
Stay?

LEONORA
Deh, fuggi!

MANRICO
No!

LEONORA
Guai se tardi!

MANRICO
No!

LEONORA
La tua vita!

MANRICO
Io la disprezzo!

LEONORA
Parti! Parti!

MANRICO
No!

LEONORA
La tua vita!

MANRICO
Io la disprezzo!
Pur...figgi, o donna,
in me gli sguardi!
Da chi l'avesti?
Ed a qual prezzo?

disc no. 2/track 21

Parlar non vuoi?
Balen tremendo!

LEONORA
Ah, flee!

MANRICO
No!

LEONORA
Woe if you delay!

MANRICO
No!

LEONORA
Your life!

MANRICO
I scorn it!

LEONORA
Leave! Leave!

MANRICO
No!

LEONORA
Your life!

MANRICO
I scorn it!
Still...O woman,
look into my eyes!
Who gave it to you?
And at what price?

You won't speak?
A terrible thought!

Dal mio rival! Intendo! Intendo!
Ha quest'infame l'amor venduto...

LEONORA
Oh quant'ingiusto!

MANRICO
Venduto un core che mio giurò!

LEONORA
Oh come l'ira ti rende cieco!
Oh quanto ingiusto, crudel, crudel...

MANRICO
Infame!

LEONORA
...sei meco! T'arrendi! Fuggi!
O sei perduto!
Nemmeno il cielo salvar ti può!

MANRICO
Ha quest'infame l'amor venduto,

LEONORA
Oh come l'ira ti rende, ti rende cieco!

MANRICO
Venduto un core che mio giurò!

LEONORA
Oh, come l'ira ti rende, ti rende cieco!

MANRICO
Infame!

From my rival! I understand!
This wretch sold her love...

LEONORA
Oh, how unjust!

MANRICO
Sold a heart sworn to me!

LEONORA
Oh, how your wrath blinds you!
Oh, how unjust and cruel you are...

MANRICO
Wretch!

LEONORA
...to me! Believe me! Flee!
Or you're lost!
Heaven itself can't save you!

MANRICO
This wretch sold her love.

LEONORA
Oh, how your wrath blinds you!

MANRICO
Sold a heart sworn to me!

LEONORA
Oh, how your wrath blinds you!

MANRICO
Wretch!

LEONORA
Oh, quanto ingiusto, crudel, crudel
sei meco! T'arrendi! Fuggi!
O sei perduto!
nemmeno il cielo salvar ti può!

MANRICO
Ha quest'infame venduto amor,
che mio giurò!

AZUCENA
Ah!
Ai nostri monti ritorneremo, ecc.

LEONORA
Ah! fuggi, fuggi! O sei perduto!
Nemmeno il cielo salvar ti può, ecc.

MANRICO
No! Ha quest'infame l'amor venduto,
venduto un cor, che mio giurò, ecc.

(Leonora sinks a Manrico's feet.)

disc no. 2/track 22

MANRICO
Ti scosta!

LEONORA
Non respingermi!
Vedi? languente,
oppressa, io manco.

MANRICO
Va! ti abomino! Ti maledico!

LEONORA
Oh, how unjust and cruel you are
to me! Believe me! Flee!
Or you're lost!
Heaven itself can't save you!

MANRICO
This wretch sold a love
sworn to me!

AZUCENA
Ah!
We'll go back to our mountains, etc.

LEONORA
Ah flee, flee! Or you're lost!
Heaven itself can't save you! etc.

MANRICO
No! This wretch sold her love,
sold a heart sworn to me, etc.

MANRICO
Go away!

LEONORA
Don't drive me off!
You see? My strength fails,
I'm overcome, weak.

MANRICO
Go! I detest you! My curse upon you!

LEONORA
Ah cessa, cessa!
Non d'imprecar,
di volgere per me la prece
a Dio è questa l'ora!

MANRICO
Un brivido corse nel petto mio!

LEONORA
Manrico!

MANRICO
Donna! svelami...narra...

LEONORA
Ho la morte in seno!

MANRICO
La morte!

LEONORA
Ah, fu più rapida
la forza del veleno ch'io non pensava!

MANRICO
Oh, fulmine!

LEONORA
Senti...la mano è gelo,
ma qui, qui foco terribil arde!

(She touches her chest.)

MANRICO
Che festi, o cielo?

LEONORA
Ah stop, stop!
Don't curse me;
the time has come
to pray to God for me!

MANRICO
A shudder runs through my breast!

LEONORA
Manrico!

MANRICO
Woman! Reveal...tell me...

LEONORA
I have death in my breast!

MANRICO
Death!

LEONORA
Ah, the poison's strength
was more rapid than I thought.

MANRICO
Oh, horror!

LEONORA
Feel...my hand is icy,
but here, here a terrible fire is burning!

MANRICO
Heaven, what have you done!

LEONORA
Prima che d'altri vivere
io volli tua morir!

MANRICO
Insano! ed io
quest'angelo osava maledir!

LEONORA
Più non resisto!

MANRICO
Ahi misera!

LEONORA
Ecco l'istante...
Io moro, Manrico.
Or la tua grazia,
padre del cielo, imploro!

MANRICO
Ciel!

LEONORA
Rather than live as another's,
I wanted to die yours!

MANRICO
And I, a madman,
dared curse this angel!

LEONORA
I can't go on!

MANRICO
Ah, hapless girl!

LEONORA
The moment has come...
I'm dying, Manrico.
Father in Heaven, now
I beg your forgiveness!

MANRICO
Heavens!

(The Count appears, stopping at the entrance)

CONTE
(Ah! volle me deludere,
e per costui morir!)

LEONORA
Prima che d'altri vivere,
io volli tua morir!

MANRICO
Insano! ed io
quest'angelo osava maledir! ecc.

COUNT
(Ah, she wanted to deceive me
and die for him!)

LEONORA
Rather than live as another's,
I wanted to die yours!

MANRICO
And I, like a madman,
dared curse this angel, etc.

LEONORA
Prima che d'altri vivere,
io volli tua morir! ecc.

CONTE
(Ah! volle me deludere,
è per costui morir! ecc.)

LEONORA
Manrico!

MANRICO
Leonora!

LEONORA
Addio! io moro!

MANRICO
Ah! Ahi, misera!

CONTE *(ai soldati)*
Sia tratto al ceppo!

MANRICO *(trascinato via)*
Madre! Ah, madre, addio!

AZUCENA
Manrico!
Ov'è mio figlio?

CONTE
A morte corre.

AZUCENA
Ah ferma! M'odi!

LEONORA
Rather than live as another's,
I wanted to die yours! etc.

COUNT
(Ah! she wanted to deceive me
and die for him! etc.)

LEONORA
Manrico!

MANRICO
Leonora!

LEONORA
Farewell, I'm dying...

MANRICO
Ah! Alas, wretched one!

COUNT *(to the soldiers)*
Take him to the block!

MANRICO *(as he is dragged off)*
Mother! Ah, Mother, farewell!

AZUCENA
Manrico!
Where is my son?

COUNT
Hastening to his death.

AZUCENA
Ah, stop! hear me!

CONTE (*la trascina alla finestra*)
Vedi!

AZUCENA
Cielo!

CONTE
È spento.

AZUCENA
Egl'era tuo fratello!

CONTE
Ei! quale orror!

AZUCENA
Sei vendicata, o madre!

CONTE
E vivo ancor!

END

COUNT (*draws her to the window.*)
See!

AZUCENA
Heaven!

COUNT
He's dead.

AZUCENA
He was your brother!

COUNT
He! What horror!

AZUCENA
Mother, you are avenged!

COUNT
And I still live!

PHOTOGRAPHY CREDITS

Il Trovatore

GIUSEPPE VERDI

COMPACT DISC ONE 71:46:00

Act One

1	All'erta! All'erta!	2:54
3	Di due figli vivea padre beato	0:44
3	Abbietta zingara, fosca vegliarda!	3:51
4	Brevi e tristi giorni visse	1:58
5	Sull'orlo dei tetti	1:26
	Ferrando/Chorus	
6	Che piú t'arresti?	2:33
	Ines/Leonora	
7	Tacea la notte	4:04
	Leonora	
8	Quanto narrasti di turbamento	0:49
9	Di tale amor	2:49
	Ines/Leonora	
10	Tace la notte!	2:08
	Conte	
11	Il Trovator! Io fremo! Deserta sulla terra	1:35
	Conte/Manrico	
12	Anima mia! Piu dell'usato	1:53
13	Di geloso amor sprezzato	2:37
	Leonora/Conte/Manrico	

Act Two

14	Anvil Chorus: Vedi! Le fosche notturne	2:57
15	Stride la vampa!	2:56

COMPACT DISC TWO   67:19:00

Act Three